SEASONS: 10 Women's Narratives on Embracing Change, Aging, and Maintaining Relevancy

ISBN   978-1-960001-37-5 (Paperback)
ISBN: 978-1-960001-38-2 (Ebook)
Library of Congress Control Number: Pending

Editor & Compiled by: Renee P. Aldrich
Proofreader: Frank Williams
Cover/Interior Design   Juan Roberts | Creative Lunacy
Literary Director: Sandra Slayton James

AUTHORS:

Renee P. Aldrich	Geraldine Massey
Patricia Armstead Daniels	Eileen Morris
Dr. Angela F. Ford	Dr. LouAnn Ross
Reverend Brenda Gregg	Terri Lynn Shields
Sharon Greene	Jennifer Cash Wade

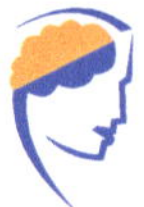

KP Publishing Company
Publisher of Fiction, Nonfiction & Children's Books
Los Angeles   •   Las Veags
www.kp-pub.com

Printed in the United States of America

TO THOSE WOMEN WHO WERE TOLD THEY ARE DONE,

because they are 60 years of age or older.

For those who were told their capacity is diminished,

FOR THOSE WHO DIDN'T KNOW HOW TO

FIGHT THOSE FALSE NARRATIVES

BUT CAN HOPEFULLY NOW HAVE A CHANGE OF PERSPECTIVE —

Enough is enough!

"Beyond
the age of 60,
women don't just endure;
we flourish,
with the wisdom
of our years
and the fire
of our determination
combined."

INTRODUCTION

Last month I turned a whopping 75 years old. When I
turned 70, I recall secretly entering a state of panic. And for the next four years, I obsessed
with the aging I was doing. (Even though over and over again I was told I didn't look a
day over 60.) During this time between the ages of 70 and 73, I literally lived each day
out loud—that would be 1,095 days of focus on age—I was sure that I had lost time. I was
running out of time; running out of time for what, you ask? Well, for all the grand and
glorious things I intended to accomplish, like getting that 750 credit score and being
credit-worthy enough to purchase my dream home.

I was running out of time to get down to a size 12/14, something I had been
aspiring to do for most of my adult life.

I felt that soon there would be no time to write that great novel, or that amazing
book of poems, or become the next Maya Angelou. (She has been gone now nine years,
and it hasn't happened yet—her replacement looks like it will be an incredibly talent-

ed young woman named Amanda Gorman). The novel would tell stories of my beloved "Soho, the community in Pittsburgh (which is now called Uptown—new name, but the fond memories linger on) where I grew up, the one that made me understand the "village" concept. (We kids were well taken care of and well parented by all the mothers in our village of Soho) I would love to have written that novel telling the amazing stories of that neighborhood, of the families, the holidays, the J&L Steel Mill Christmas parties, the summers at Kennywood Park as a full community, the dances at South Park Barn with our Vacation Bible School group when someone would be on the outside keeping guard that Reverend Jones didn't come down and catch us dancing. The book of poetry would be a volume filled with beautiful and thoughtful prose on important topics such as love, joy, sorrow, social ills, and "Peace in the World." I could have written volumes of stories about that precious time that sped by so quickly. But here I was, 70 plus, and I had run out of time for all these possibilities.

Now hold on, I know what you are thinking, and believe me, I am aware in my heart that I should have been shouting to the heavens, thanking God over and over again for the blessing of having lived this long, long enough to see my children become productive adults, to have a beautiful grandson—and to see him turn five and be brilliant beyond measure. And indeed, I fully understand that it was through God's grace and mercy that here I stood in my 70s, still in relatively good health, with my faculties intact and functioning in a way that allows me to still take care of myself, make a living, travel, and be a blessing to others from time to time. Yet, I spent much of my time angsting about aging in terms of "what things I haven't done, what I don't look like, and what I don't have."

Finally, a friend suggested that I stop lamenting and put some action behind it. (I won't say her name, but her initials are Tammy T. Thompson, Executive Director of Catapult Pittsburgh.) She insisted to me that perhaps some others were in the same head space, and perhaps I could design some conversations within my program, Softer Side Seminars, for women my age who were struggling with these same issues and who may be able to benefit from workshops around the pressure of aging.

After I shook off the impact (self-pity) of my friend not giving me any energy on my perspective—I realized she was correct and began to process a way to do that.

Softer Side Seminars, the Empowerment and Self Esteem program I was called to start in 2002, was about to be 20 years old. It occurred to me that I needed to recognize the date with a positive reflection of my being 20 years older than I was at that time and include the voices of my peers, who were with me in one way or the other over this time, who were also 20 years older. And this is what this volume represents.

It is a collection of narratives written by women, most of whom have been friends of mine over the entire time, some newer friends, but all of whom are over the age of 60, have made tremendous contributions to their community, still in the market place, have faced some adversity--some more than others—have had to make changes, and make some difficult choices. Still, mostly the essays show these women are overcomers.

They offer words of wisdom and show strength but are not afraid of being vulnerable in willingness to be transparent about issues and weaknesses. More than this, they demonstrate who we seasoned women are as a populace, still bring much to the table, and remain relevant in all areas. We command and deserve respect and recognition that we are not diminished in capacity—physical or mental.

I pray you read these essays and they feed your spirits.

And if in some way you fall into the headspace I was in, or if you feel the pangs of aging (even though you give thanks to God every day for every moment of your life), or if you are subject to the negative definition that society, unevolved family members, or those who don't know their time is coming, try to place on you; do not buy into it.

Do not accept it as your reality. Read these essays and know that you still got it; you are amazing, there is value in your journey, and you don't have to stop until the Lord says so.

— Renee P. Aldrich

*"Mostly,
what I have learned so
far about aging, despite
the creakiness of one's
bones and cragginess of
one's once-silken skin,
is this:
Do it, By all means, Do it."*

— Maya Angelou

FOREWORD

DR. KATHY W. HUMPHREY
President, Carlow University,
Pittsburgh, Pennsylvania

In the tapestry of life, there are individuals who rise above the ordinary, illuminating the path for others through their unwavering dedication, vision, and compassion. We celebrate the extraordinary legacy of a woman whose impact has transformed countless lives. Renee Aldrich, the visionary behind "Softer Side Seminars," stands as a shining example of what one individual can achieve when fueled by a deep commitment to empower, educate, and uplift others.

This book is not just a collection of essays but a testament to the power of transformation, resilience, and the enduring spirit of sisterhood. Within these pages, we embark on a deeply personal and transformative voyage, guided by nine remarkable women's wisdom, grace, and unwavering resiliency.

The essays within this collection weave a tapestry of experiences that transcend time. They reveal the early life of each author—an intimate glimpse into the formative years that laid the foundation for the extraordinary women they would become.

We walk beside them through the terrain of teenage dreams and the challenges of early adulthood, witnessing the evolution of aspirations and the forging of indomitable spirits.

These women have not merely lived their lives; they have courageously embraced life and transformation. We journey with them through the chapters of their marriages, professional careers, and the relationships that have shaped their identities. From the pulpit to the boardroom, from the realm of healthcare to the world of entrepreneurship, their paths have been diverse, inspiring, and a testament to the endless possibilities that await those who dare to dream.

As we delve into their narratives, we gain insight into their reflections on aging—an often misunderstood aspect of life. These women dispel the myths and stereotypes, teaching us that aging is not a journey into the shadows but rather a path to greater wisdom, self-discovery, and, ultimately, the light. With each passing year, they have accumulated not only memories but also profound insights and a deeper understanding of what it means to truly live.

Their essays offer a gift to younger generations—a treasure trove of wisdom, a roadmap for navigating life's complexities with authenticity and perseverance. These women have walked boldly through the storms of adversity, emerging not as victims of circumstance but as triumphant heroes of their own stories. They generously share the wealth of insight they have gathered along the way.

These narratives do not shy away from the tensions and challenges of life. With vulnerability and candor, the authors reveal the trials they have faced and the methodologies they have employed to overcome them. They speak of the pivotal role faith has played in their journeys—a source of strength, solace, and unwavering resolve.

Renee's vision, embodied in "Softer Side Seminars," has not only provided a platform for these remarkable women to share their stories but has also nurtured a community of empowerment and sisterhood. Through her tireless efforts, she has sown the seeds of transformation, fostering a legacy that will continue to bear fruit for generations to come.

As you turn the pages of "Seasons," may you be inspired by these remarkable women's strength, resilience, and enduring spirit. Their stories are a testament to the boundless possibilities that await us all as we navigate the ever-changing seasons of life.

Congratulations to Renee Aldrich and the nine extraordinary authors who have contributed their voices to this collection—Reverend Brenda Gregg, Dr. Angela Ford, Eileen Morris, Terri Lynn Shields, Jennifer Cash Wade, Dr. Lou Ann Ross, Geraldine Massey, Sharon Greene, and Patricia Armstead Daniels. Your stories are a source of inspiration and empowerment, and your legacy will continue to uplift and guide women around the world.

— Dr. Kathy W. Humphrey

"Age is
but a number;
the spirit of a mature
woman is timeless,
radiating confidence
and wisdom
in every step
she takes."

TABLE *of* CONTENTS

JENNIFER CASH WADE

Real Estate Agent
Pittsburgh, Pennsylvania

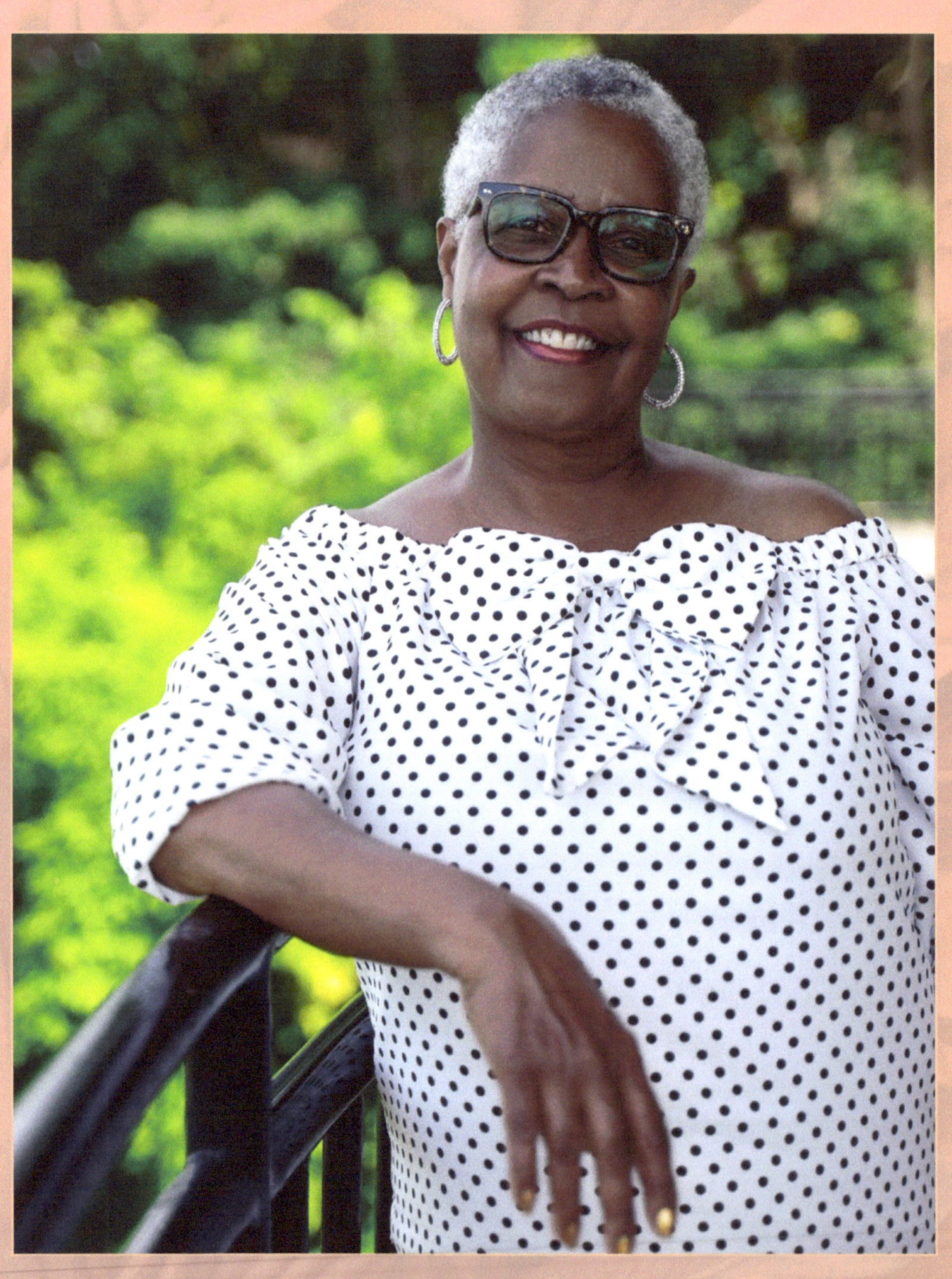

The Circle *of* Life

August 23, 1948–I never knew the time or the day of the week, but that is the date I entered this world seventy-four years ago in all my glory! My parents loved telling the story of my arrival of how my mom went into labor, my dad went to get a cab to take her to the hospital, when he returned, I was there to greet him!

Calvin and Dorothy Cash named me Jennifer Harriet Cash. At the time of my birth, we lived in the historic Hill District with my older sister, Clarissa, and thirteen months later our younger brother, Calvin, joined the family. We lived at 1415 Webster Avenue for the first six years of my life before we were forced to move to allow for the construction of the Civic Arena. A few days before Thanksgiving of 1954, we moved to Beltzhoover in a lovely little red brick house that my parents purchased where 827 Ashdale Street would be their home for the rest of their lives.

I grew up in a traditional, two parent home, with four brothers, a sister, and myself. My mom did not work outside the home, until she went to school to become an LPN—when she graduated, she was pregnant with their fourth child—a brother who was 11 years younger than me. His birth was followed three years later by twin boys. Mother

Cash ended her nursing career as a private duty nurse 25 years after receiving her license. She went back to being a homemaker and then a first lady supporting her husband in the ministry. She passed away at the age of 87. My mother was kind, gentle, and a true class act. She was a great lover of people also, and I am sure I inherited some of my empathic ways from her. In her heart she truly believed that no matter what, there was always some good to be found in every person, and she therefore responded to everyone with that attitude. And she loved the Lord, totally and completely.

My father was employed at H.H. Robertson Company, an international manufacturing firm where he worked for 40 years before retiring. After his retirement, my dad received the call to ministry, and would serve as a preacher of the Gospel for over 20 years. He also got involved with community work at the tender age of 80, working to install cutting edge technology in his church. A geo-thermal heating and cooling system that would use run off mine water as its source of energy to heat and cool the church, John Wesley on Herron Avenue in the historic Hill District. Pastor Cash lived until he was nine days shy of his 92nd birthday.

Now, at age 75, I am grateful for the life I enjoy and fully embrace my status as a senior citizen. I've always looked at "getting older" as the natural order of things, so if asked my feelings about aging, my response will always be positive, full of joy and committed to being all that God has designed me to be.

In all honesty, I can say I have never felt age-conscious. Even as I grow older and begin to experience "new" things like aches & pains for no apparent reason or realize that some tasks now take longer to complete, I recognize them as part of the process and make the changes necessary in my everyday life to accommodate them.

Because I fully embrace the circle of life, I don't allow the behavior of others, nor negative attitudes toward senior individuals, to become an issue for me. I simply remind myself that if they are fortunate enough to live long, rich lives they, too, will experience those same behaviors or attitudes directed towards them!

The feelings of confidence and self-worth my parents instilled in me coupled with life experiences and opportunities I've been given have enabled me to develop a healthy attitude about what it means to age, and to effectively handle any situations that may challenge my age.

When I think about qualities that have helped define me and create the space for me to navigate through my life, one I believe that is most valuable is that I connect well with people, and have always had a knack for making sure people feel seen and valued. I remember during my training to become a reservations agent with Trans World Airlines (TWA), our instructor noticed a young lady in our class who seemed to be struggling and was falling behind. At the same time, she noticed the way I seemed to be able to easily interact with everyone in our small intimate group, so she asked me to talk with my classmate and offer to help her. I did and she opened up to me thankful that someone cared enough to offer to help. She was able to catch up, moved through the rest of the training with ease and secured a permanent position with the rest of our class.

I have always had a heart for people and have never been afraid to step in and fight for various causes that may have negatively impacted them. I am fiercely protective of my family and will always be. When I was younger, I was known to speak up for a person if they were not speaking for themselves. I have the capacity to feel pain and joy of others, and am driven to making sure that when I interact with people on any level, I make them feel "okay" about something. In turn, it spills over into my spirit, and I am better because of it.

The foundation in our home was the key instrument that helped form the woman I have become. This includes the fact that I was a high academic achiever. I was always in advanced classes throughout my school years. In our home our education was a non-negotiable, my parents insisted upon excellence in school; meaning we had to clearly demonstrate that we were doing our absolute best. This was important because it was a time a lot of school districts were experiencing racial tensions. And while there were a lot of white students and white teachers in our school, I can honestly say the Black students were not overlooked. They worked to bring out the best in all of us—we were supported and encouraged on all points.

Regrettably there were scenarios in school that, did not always reflect a "treat everyone fairly" mentality. I really wanted to be a cheerleader, subsequently I tried out many times—every year. For some reason, the woman who was selecting would never pick me. Even though I was never a cheerleader, I still wanted to be a part of that environment, so I made sure I stayed involved in whatever they were doing. If there was an event, I'd always volunteer to help out. On one of these occasions, the woman who never would pick me, saw me working at an event and said, "Oh there's Jennifer again always passing out cookies and punch." Now can you imagine how that could have devastated my fourteen-year-old psyche? It is a good thing that I was fortunate enough to have a strong sense of self and I never gave her remarks any of my energy.

I've always been blessed with a happy spirit, that spirit opened doors for me, and drew people to me. Even as a teen, I had the privilege of selling lunch tickets in the school cafeteria and that was so fun for me. I don't quite recall how I got that special job, but I do know, that I'd sit in a cage, selling the tickets for every lunch period. I think one of the reasons it was so great is because you got out of class—to make it all the more valid for me is that it was a paying job. Each Friday I'd make my way to the back of the cafeteria to the dietician's little office where she'd have an envelope containing my "pay." It was probably no more than $10, but it gave me a such a major sense of accomplishment. Yes, I'd say my childhood was sprinkled with things that brought me joy, and added to the natural joy I always seemed to have.

My integral part of background included the community outside my household and it contributed greatly to the nurturing I received. I was raised in the very neighborhood I live in now, Beltzhoover—belts'hoover—specifically on a street called Ashdale. While Beltzhoover was a wonderful family-oriented community, it was Ashdale Street that was our village in and of itself. Everyone on Ashdale was a family, a mother, father, and children. Even though our street was tucked away, each family was connected to the other, we played at night, it was safe, we were in and out of each other's home and it was an amazing kinship that existed there. The entire neighborhood of Beltzhoover was self-contained. We had an A&P, a shoe shop, a doctor, a drugstore—everything we needed essentially. And it was all surrounded by McKinley Park. This was the loving, supportive community that helped turned us into self-sufficient adults.

My professional life has afforded me many opportunities for continued learning and emotional development. Back in the day, most young ladies right out of high school were "tray girls" at local hospitals. I did that as a first adult job. I trained with TWA, and I alternated between the TWA training program and nursing school and ended up getting a nursing degree and becoming an RN. I soon discovered that nursing was not for me, so I kept the reservationist job with TWA. I also did a stint with Bell Telephone or today it's known as AT&T.

One of my father's duties at H.H. Robertson was travel coordinator. That afforded him the opportunity to meet Alex and Rhoda Zelenski who owned Mon Valley Travel, a vacation travel agency. They wanted to add a corporate division to their agency and wanted my dad to manage it on a part-time basis. He agreed and as a result of his work with them, he brought my then husband on as a sales manager. I joined the agency later after taking a six-year work hiatus to care for our children. I stayed in the travel business for over fifteen years.

I looked at all of these experiences as contributors to my personal evolution. They left me better off than I was when I started—better because I came away with new knowledge and new relationships. And an important aspect of achieving success in life is making and cultivating good relationships.

However, It would be the real estate industry that would advance me the most.

When I got into real estate, that was the leap of a lifetime. I entered at the recruitment of another agent who hired me to be her assistant. I did this for a moment, but after a short while, I knew that being an assistant would not serve me well. I wanted to build my own clientele, and grow my business—so I did.

There were numerous struggles associated with this decision because I was essentially starting from scratch. I had three sons by this time, my husband and I had divorced, and I had no other income. Part of the struggle included losing my car, but I was determined, and took the bus until I was able to purchase another car and began to move my real estate business towards success.

The acquisition of wisdom comes from the collection of life experiences, that include good ones and bad ones. It includes getting things right and making mistakes. The most important thing about making mistakes, or facing challenging times is the "learning" that can come from them. I have learned a great deal from each experience, and I choose to be grateful for the teaching that came from getting through things.

As a result, I learned I am able to help others learn. I believe it is our job as older women to teach younger women and instill things in them that they are willing to embrace and can use in their lives. I firmly believe that there is a lot to be said about how things used to be—in how we parent, run our homes, and present ourselves.

Therefore, I share with my granddaughters, my daughter-in-law, my nieces, and even young women in the neighborhood. I am blessed to have something to share, or some direction to offer. My mother used to always tell me she'd say, "You know people are watching you, you may not know it, but they are." She shared that I was setting an example. As I've had many things to overcome, or push through, she was advising me that I had to operate with grace—conduct myself, regardless of the situation, with class.

I offer to younger women, to get the lesson, when life happens, and you go through things—and you will go through things—whatever you do, get the lesson. Additionally, it is important to remember that the best pathway towards happiness, is adjusting your attitude. I know it is a cliché, but the question of the view of the glass must be considered—what do you see? A glass that is half empty or one that is half full? Mine has always been half full. And are you making lemonade out of those lemons, or just giving up and complaining because they are sour?

What I do know for sure is that we serve ourselves better when we look for the "good" in things, rather than become overwhelmed by the negative that exists. Not from a Pollyanna mentality that states "everything and everyone is good all the time," but understanding there are negative things that are completely out of our control, and choosing that we won't be negatively impacted because of them.

At the end of the day, I know that I know that I know my capacity comes from Him, and that is what I would share with younger women. Time will pass, you'll find that youth will escape you, but it is only the number that has changed, your capacity comes from God, trust Him, talk to Him, and then listen for His direction. You can never go wrong with that.

Jesus loves you and so do I! My mother, Mother Dorothy Cash always told me this and it has always and uplifted me. I pray it does likewise for you. **JCW**

"In the
tapestry of life,
a mature woman's
threads shimmer with
experience, weaving tales
of resilience, strength,
and
unwavering faith."

REVEREND BRENDA GREGG

Pastor, Destiny of Faith Church,
Founder, Project Destiny, Inc.
Pittsburgh, Pennsylvania

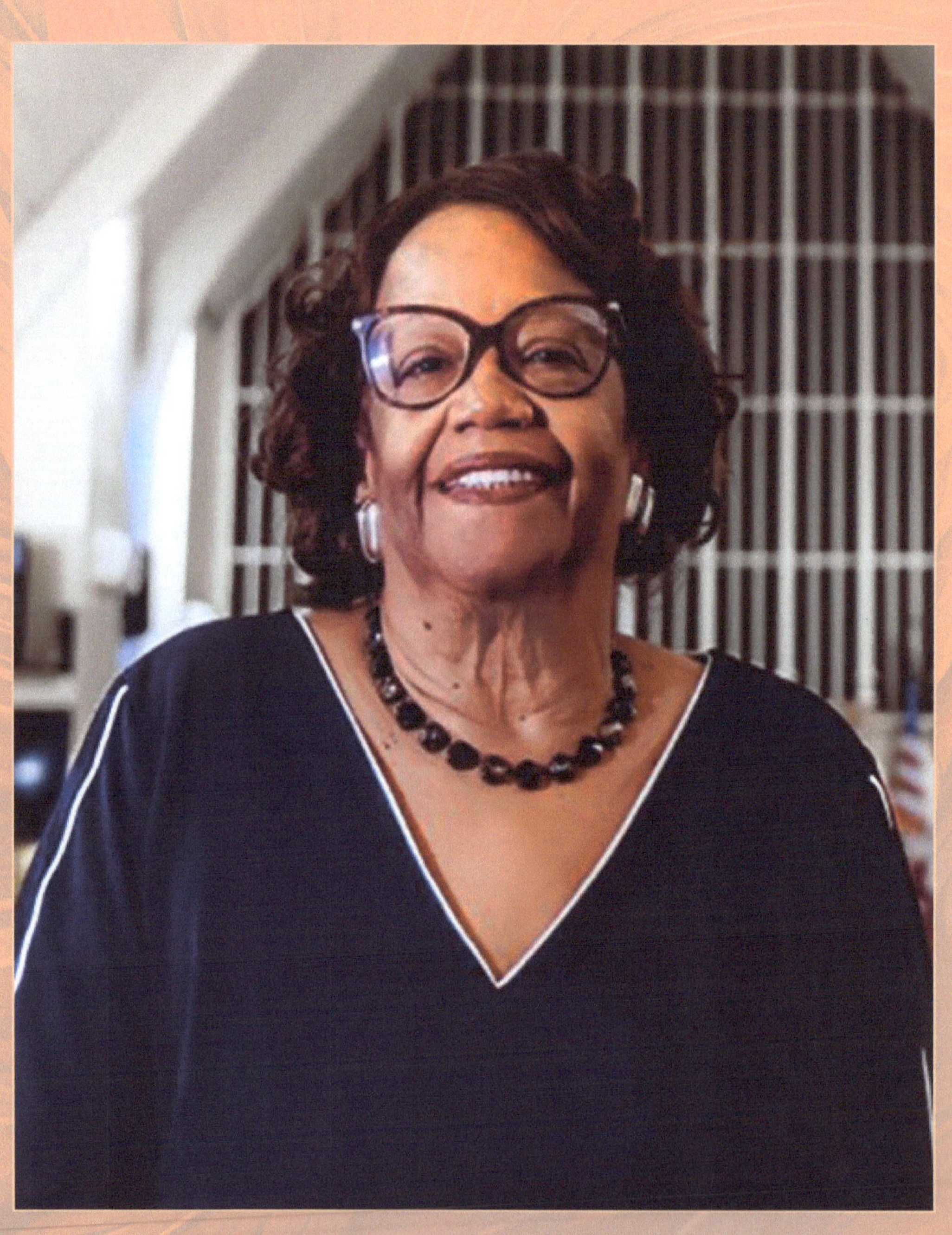

Seasons *of* My Life — Walk Into Your Season

Very recently, my five-year-old granddaughter was behind me, as we walked up the steps to the second floor of my house. Falling is something I have always been fearful of, especially, as I have grown older. I spent one of my major careers as a health care administrator, but you don't have to be a hospital administrator to know that falls are one of the most common, costly, and harmful health outcomes across settings of care. Statistics have it that there are millions of people who fall each day of the year. Thousands of dollars are spent per fall. I have seen the devastation of an aged person who experiences a fall. So, my walk is different, especially as I climb the stairs at the wonderful age of 73 years old.

Kyla, my bright inquisitive granddaughter, who is not yet aware of the dangers of falling, asks me this question, "Grammy, why do you walk this way up the steps?"

Instead of sharing with her my fear of falling, I asked her a few questions instead. "Kyla, what do you mean? How am I walking?" She was not the least bit hesitant at all, in showing me what she meant and fashioning for me how I looked as I climbed those stairs. She swiftly stepped around me to show me. She said, "Grammy, you walk up the stairs and even down the stairs one step at a time. You move one foot and don't move the other foot until your second foot is on the same step. It takes you a long time to get up and down the stairs."

I decided to ask her another question. "Kyla, how should I walk up these stairs?" She began to climb one step at a time but not at all trying to balance herself with the other foot, if she could have, she would have taken two steps at a time. She said, "Grammy, this is the way you should walk up the stairs." All I could say is, "Really Kyla…are you for real? For real?"

A few days later, after that scene had taken place, I began to share what Kyla said to me with her mother who is in her early thirties. She responded to me and said, "She'll learn Mom, it is all about the aging seasons in life." There was so much spoken and unspoken being said in those words exchanged between the three generations of women in my life.

It is all about the seasons and walking one step at a time. Sure, there were certainly times when I thought I could skip a few steps to get where I thought I wanted to go. But God, more times than a few, had to stop me, as Kyla did to question my actions, my motives, and the choices that I have found myself engulfed in.

I realized that there is so much we don't understand when we are young. But just let the Lord give us some additional time, a second chance to get things right, and we begin to learn that we must take one step at a time. We appreciate it a bit more as we age, grow up, mature, and develop in those teaching moments each season affords us. The seasons can't be denied as being the real educator, or teachers, of our lives.

There is so much I have learned, both good and bad, as I walked by sight rather than by faith. We see a lot of things, we go after so much and the things we see sometimes, in our early life, are things we try to achieve from our seeing, and yet we are not ready to achieve what we see because sometimes it takes walking by faith rather than walking by sight. It takes climbing that stairway to heaven one step at a time, with all the stairway's twists and turns.

The early season of my life came when I was only 19 when I married my husband, who was a Baptist minister, ready to move into his pastoral career. I was a young woman who loved ministry. My husband and I grew up in the same church, sat under the same pastor who married us, and blessed our first-born son two years later. So here I was in my early twenties, married to a young minister, and the mother of a precious son while working full time. My husband's only desire was to preach the gospel, even if this work put very little food on our table. He tried to work several jobs, but his heart was not in it.

So, I learned early into our marriage that I would need a career that could help feed our family. Working hard was not a hardship for me, since I grew up in a family who worked hard as both my parents were excellent examples of this. My father worked in the steel mill for most of his adult life. Dad was an experienced construction worker who could and did build houses or anything else he had to. He was meticulous in everything he did.

I was used to seeing him work hard, work different shifts, and shift quickly when he had to. Hard seasons as a steel worker came often with layoffs. He would travel down south to work in his family's construction business to keep food on our table and a roof over our heads. My father was so proud and excited to build a new home for my mother before his retirement. He built the new house but died seven years later at 59 years old before he could receive Social Security and his retirement. This was one of those sad seasons in our lives.

My mother had the same work ethic as my father. She was a domestic worker and she cleaned "white peoples" houses when I was young. In fact, she would take me with her when school was out, to help her. She found me one of my first jobs; working all summer at a house where there were two little white boys that I cared for, made their lunches, and cleaned their house. I loved the kids but knew this was not how I was going to make a living. But this was a season of preparation.

My mother eventually got a position at a nearby hospital where she stayed until she retired to take care of her own elderly mother. My mother passed at the wonderful age of 83 and she never remarried.

So, I have had the opportunity of watching closely at generational seasonal changes in not only my family but also in me. I had such strong role models. I would not be what I am today if it wasn't for my mother and father pressing through their own seasonal changes in front of my sister and me. They had such dignity and self-esteem no matter what season they were in.

SEASONS

I've done what I saw my parents do. I did many things like clean houses, babysat other people's children, cashiered at a grocery store, and worked 38 years in healthcare where I climbed the career ladder to vice president while raising my three children, attending college, entering the ministry as a single woman, and pastoring three churches in a major denomination and being appointed presiding elder for nineteen churches in Ohio. Sometimes God will send you to a place that is hard. Being in Ohio with no consistent place to lay my head. It was my season to leave the place I loved so much and travel weekly to where I needed to be, sleeping at the seminary when I had to, staying in hotels, and using my last dime just to put gas in my car. But God! He makes a way out of no way! People use these words but, oh how true they really were to me.

I have retired several times and yet I have never stopped working. I am and have been the founder and executive director of a non-profit organization since 2004. This business employs over 45 people on staff, mostly full-time minority employees made up of many are single mothers and fathers who live and work in the community. They are strong people who have been through their own seasons and now are helping others to get through theirs. Look at what God can do!

You would think that I would stop working, go home and sit down, collect that little amount of Social Security and become an AARP member with joy and satisfaction. I've earned my time to stop working and take it easy. Why can't I stop and just do the things I want to do? Instead of sitting down and resting, I was called to plant a new congregation in the inner city where I have been and remain the senior pastor for the past 11 years.

I have been blessed by God to do many things while still having the strength and the mental capacity to do more. And I forgot to mention that six years ago, I received a diagnosis that I had breast cancer. Another new season that I personally had never experienced before. I couldn't imagine I had breast cancer. I had a church to pastor, and I had an agency to lead. I felt great and I had prayed and walked seven other women through their illness of breast cancer in a short period of time. But now, how was I to get through my own season of breast cancer, doctor visits, radiation treatments, and taking more medicine than I had ever taken in my life and do what I knew I was not finished doing. It is never over until God says it's over.

I share all of this with you to confirm that many seasons come and go. You never know where life is taking you. But one thing I do know, that through each one of the seasons that I have gone through, it has been God who has kept me each step of the way.

All of us, go through different seasons in our life.

Thinking of my seasons—the good and the bad, my ups and my downs. Seasons change and difficulties, struggle and fears do come. I am always reminded that "God has not given me the spirit of fear but instead He has given me power, love and a sound mind." When you get to the place where I am right now, I am thankful for my sound mind! Can I get a witness?

I have experienced my own winter, spring, summer, and fall and I realize that there is still so much to do. I know for sure I will not be doing the same things I have done in the early years of my life, but I am also clear as I have had the joy to work beside so many skilled and God-loving ministers, administrative individuals and staff who are paid and those who give of their time and expertise. So, I am now 73 years old, cancer-free, single, pastor, teacher, administrator, mother, grandmother, and friend. God has kept me, and I am still here.

More than anything else, I listen more closely for and to the voice of God and I let God lead me in the path of righteousness for His name's sake, not for my own selfish needs to be met. I want and need the Lord to lead me as I step into this new season of my life at the wonderful age of 73 years old.

I have always been challenged by the work I have done, and I have never been afraid to try new things to move forward I have learned to do all I can do to follow the commands, prompting, and voice of God. And that means no matter how I love what I have been able to do and accomplish over the years, I know that at the end of the day, it's all about God's seasonal change and direction. He is the master, He is the captain of my ship, He holds the reins in the power of His almighty hand, and we are His stewards. He knows what is best for His Kingdom. He knows what is best for me and He is also the one who directs each one of our steps.

So, in this final season, I am still here and while still here I want more than anything else, to make good use of the season where I am right now. I've learned from my past but there is still a future for me, even now.

In this season, I look ahead, and I search for the "ones" God directs and sends my way. I want more than anything else to be able to pour oil into a new and younger generation. What I have done needs this next generation to carry it on in ways that I can never even imagine. And I believe I have what it takes to step into this new and, what could be for me, my final season diligently, into the process without fear or anxiety for God truly knows what is best for me and the family that God has placed into my life. I want to be available to them because as I see what I see, the enemy is really after our seed and our seed's seed.

Think about that and know that the enemy would like to kill and destroy all that God has created, built, and developed. It's time that I can gracefully move over and work God's work a different way, His way. So, while I am still here and while I still have my sound mind, I will work doing something meaningful, expressive and purposeful. I am still planning, I am still working, I am still enjoying my life and what I can do as I walk out my season one step at a time. Yes, that is exactly what I am now planning to do, transitioning without kicking and screaming. I will someday transition into real retirement and will continue walking clearly into a season of unceasing prayer. I am praying, I am seeking wise counsel from those I respect who believe that God has called me to move forward and step into serving Him in a fresh and different way.

"For I know the thoughts that I think toward you, saith the Lord, thoughts of peace, and not of evil, to give you an expected end." Jeremiah 29:11 (KJV)

I continue to live by my favorite scripture that reminds me daily, "I can do all things through Christ who strengths me." **RBG**

"Maturity
brings with it
a unique kind of beauty
— one that is grounded in
self-awareness, spiritual
depth, and the knowledge
that a woman's value only
grows with time."

EILEEN J. MORRIS

Artistic Director, Ensemble Theater
Houston, Texas

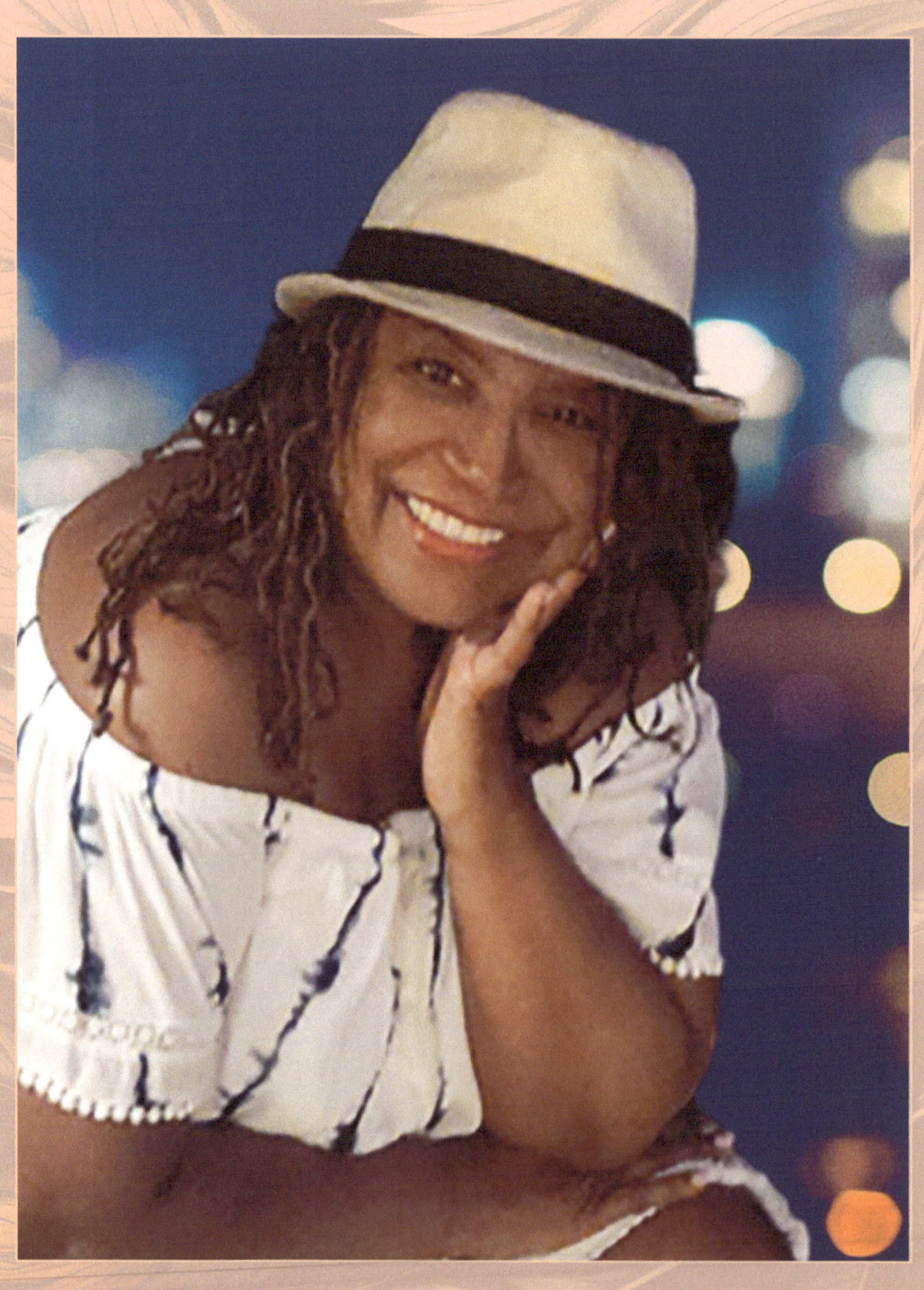

Purpose—Passion—Power
Perfect Recipe for Life—At Any Age

My given name is Eileen Maria Teresa Johnson Morris, I am the daughter of Imelda Maria Teresa Dorian Johnson Benson and James Roosevelt Johnson. My ancestors come out of Lafayette and Opelousas, Louisiana. I was born and raised in Chicago, Illinois but my parents moved us to the country town of Pembroke Township, 60 miles south of Chicago when I was five. This was a predominately Black community where people lived trying to create a better life for their families. They wanted to raise us in an environment that would be healthy, not dangerous and provide a place for us to play and grow. Thus, we moved from the west side of Chicago where gangs prevailed, to ten acres of land where we truly learned how to raise farm animals like cows, hogs, chickens, ducks and grow vegetables.

We built our own home, a three-bedroom house with a full basement of cedar blocks, and it was there that I hold my most cherished memories. We were referred to as the "Johnson family that lived up on the hill." Our parents sent all six children to Catholic school from pre-K through high school. Now you know we really couldn't afford tuition for that many kids, so on Saturdays we ALL cleaned the church to help offset the tuition.

My parents wanted us to have the same opportunities that any Caucasian child could get so, if we were in the environment with them, then "Sister Veronica" and "Father Alexander" would have to teach me and my siblings the very same way they taught little "Susie" since we'd be sitting in the seat right besides she, and little "Timmy."

It became the philosophical approach of our parents: You are given the opportunity to be your best, now you must do your best in all ways. We were encouraged to participate in numerous school activities from spelling bees to opportunities that led to receiving the American Legion Award, and school plays—even when they felt you couldn't audition or be Snow White because you weren't white. Consequently, I became a girl scout, I played volleyball, softball, ran track, and played clarinet, and participated in the school band. Also, I was a co-founder of the first ever Afro-American club in our high school. It was instilled in us that with your education and extra-curricular activities, we were to be of service. I joined the Pembrook Community choir, and also would sing in high school and college. While doing so I honed my singing and presentation skills, and at the same time I was able to gain exposure to more denominations of churches outside of Catholicism. Additionally, I began tutoring English and math at eleven years old at the public library to adults. Our parents insisted that we exemplify courage, honor, leadership, patriotism, scholarship, and service. The qualities that an American Legion award recipient displayed.

On top of this we learned how to milk cows, kill chickens for food, and grow vegetables. Understanding how the earth provides all that we need. The saying, "What a man," or in this case, a woman, "sows is what he shall reap." What you want your future to become determines what you will do today." My family lives by the principles of the African Ghanaian Sankofa bird, "go back to the past and bring forward that which is useful in your present."

We would travel at least once a year from Illinois to Houston, Texas to visit our maternal and paternal grandparents and other relatives. It is those trips that set the stage for my brothers, sister and me to move as adults from Illinois to Houston in the mid-1980s. On one of my visits to Houston before we moved, I met The Ensemble Theatre founder, George Hawkins, and my love for theatre kicked in, and my passion ignited. He saw something in me that I didn't see in myself. While earning my degree in theatre, all I wanted to do was act, yet my background was preparing me for a journey that I never thought I would experience. George hired me to become his managing director of The Ensemble Theatre.

I learned to create budgets, prepare contracts, grant writing, the fiscal management of the institution, all while being led to understand the dynamics of running a non-profit, Black institution. When George made his transition in 1990, I became the artistic director and became engaged fully in creating the art, choosing artists, actors, designers, directors, crew, the plays, choosing community-centric relationships, and working closely with the board, etc. The world of artistic directing in the 1990's and even up until a few years ago, was predominately male dominated. I was one of a handful of women who carried that torch. Many times, I would have to stand up for my beliefs and uphold women's issues, crying out for recognition so that our voices could be heard. I am very proud to have done that, not because of me, but for those whom I know will come after me.

I aimed in my leadership to find avenues in which women's voices could be heard and recognized for their excellence. I began seeking more women playwrights, directors, designers, and staff. I remember specifically reaching out to artists such as August Wilson and Ntozake Shange asking them to allow The Ensemble Theatre to produce their work and be impactful in how our art would be presented. In 2018, I read about an opportunity to apply for a $250K grant for artistic women leaders, so I applied even though the odds were against me but doing a thing "scared" proved to make me a winner. I became one of the initial groups of five women who in these past five years has received $1.25 million dollars to support women's initiatives from the BOLD Theater Leadership Circle.

The only women of color as a part of the initial cohort, I am the only woman in the world that has directed eight of the August Wilson Pittsburgh cycle plays. I have two of his pieces left to become the first woman to direct all ten plays. The Ensemble Theatre owns its own building and is the largest in the southwest and the third largest financial Black theatre in the world. This is a testament to the dedication, tenacity and passion passed down from our founder and given to generations of artists. I can't help but think about the woman I am today without thinking about the foundation provided to me by my parents and grandparents, the village, our community that helped me to be.

SEASONS

You can't get through this life without facing trials, and unfortunately, I have had my share. But through it all, I am most grateful, thankful, for the love and commitment that has been shown to me by so many.

I often was considered an overachiever. I finished high school in three and a half years. Today that is normal but in the 1970s it wasn't. I entered college and was determined to do the same thing, so at 19 years old, while taking 21 hours of college credits. However, in my second year of, my world became altered as my maternal grandfather, Lee Dorian Sr. died, and my mother and father divorced after 26 years of marriage. I felt defeated. But even then, I knew that defeat was not an option. And it wasn't. I worked hard and finished college the following year, and true to form, graduated in just over three years, got married and worked creating programs for youth. Though I wasn't in my dream job yet I was still moving toward it. My husband and I moved to Houston, where I met George and as I mentioned, my life was changed forever. In 1999, my husband and I divorced after 21 years of marriage, my dream job in theatre decided they wanted to go in another direction and my only grandson was born. These were hard blows to my world. But perseverance pays off in so many ways.

In 1999, I moved to Pittsburgh, Pennsylvania and began the healing process for myself. I began working closely with one of my few female mentors, Dr. Vernell A. Watson Lillie, at the Kuntu Repertory Theatre at the University of Pittsburgh, as her managing director. I learned more about who I was as a woman, as a Black woman, my culture, from her and August Wilson and ultimately directed in variety of theatres in Pittsburgh. Because of my commitment to the Arts, and my push for excellence, I garnered a reputation of producing art that truly mimicked life, as Rob Penny used to say.

With all these great achievements going on, it was during this time that my greatest challenge of all time happened, my only child and son, Alex Jr., was arrested for murder. This was a whole new level of devastation and my entire world was turned upside down. For the next 19 years we would fight with appeals, lawyers, and cries for justice. Pushing through these circumstances, meant refusing to give up or give in to the detriment of the situation. No, never, ever as I learned that to overcome a crisis, you need to fully commit to finding a way forward. You must approach the problem with determination and motivation. This mindset requires you have a willingness to stare adversity in the face.

In the meantime, I was asked to return to Houston to once again and become the artistic director of The Ensemble Theatre. What a full circle moment that was. It was in 2006, and as God would have it, I could still do the work I love, I was able to be with my family and assist in the caregiving of my ninety-year-old active mother. By 2023, Alex Jr. just made parole and came home March 22. I am moving toward the next chapter in my life that brings me joy and fulfills my passion. I am a witness that the rough roads we crossover do indeed make us stronger. Though it is difficult to see when we are going through, but when we stop and pause—which we must—you can see, feel, and believe it. As my mother is often quoted saying, "This too shall pass."

When I think about my personal aging journey, as an African American woman, I'm genetically predisposed to "make it." And I believe the saying, "Good Black don't crack." When I recall the road of our ancestors, age was not a factor with them. God brought them through, and they did not have half the modern amenities we have. With His continued blessings, we can do anything. Today, I still stand on the shoulders of my ancestors, I acknowledge and am thankful to those whose footsteps that I follow. What they did influences me and makes a difference in everything that I do—from volunteer projects, board positions, directing theatrical productions to serving on various panels and representing myself as a Black woman in the arts. My thought will be always never ever give up, I'm all in—and why wouldn't I be? I am blessed with a career that brings me joy and laughter, and at the same time embraces challenges, over which I have fiscal responsibility, and still fuels my passion, in a field I love. And what's more, through the arts, I can deliver the same to the world.

I would recommend some things to the women coming behind me. First and foremost, try with all your might to end up with work/career you are passionate about— that was my best gift from God other than my life, was showing me early where my passion lies—in theatre. I think often about my maternal grandmother and her words to me, when she found out that I was majoring in theatre. She was a Creole woman and often said to me, "Oh but ma chez, why you wanna waste your mama's money." I wish that my grandmother who we lovingly called "Nanny" could see that I have spent my entire life doing what I love—creating and making theatre art—and that it indeed was not a waste at all.

One outstanding part to my role has been that it has allowed me to be a mentor to both women and men especially those in theatre. A few thoughts I've shared with them: don't take no for an answer, if you get a "no"—ask again, try again, know your worth, put your big girl or big boy underwear on and just make it happen, fear is not an option, so don't allow it to take over.

Being a compassionate listener has been my best offering. I have found that people need that more than anything. I may give advice, but more than anything, I am willing to listen—I find that once people know they are heard, they will lean into you better. As women, listening is an essential trait. Because we are generally the organizers of our homes and in most workplaces, it's our listening skill that keeps things smooth as this is heavy in the theatre.

Take focus on organizing your life, think:

1 If I could share with young women getting their footing in life, I would say to them. Write in your journal, outline a one-year, three, and five-year plan. If that is too daunting, doing it in six-month increments. You should look at everything as a learning opportunity. Be sure to nurture important relationships, as they will carry you for the rest of your life.

2 Stay the course and never every give up. Keep patient. I have recently been in a situation of dealing with my ex-husband's current spouse. My son, Alex Jr., has recently been released after nineteen years of incarceration, and his dad came to visit him as he wanted to share love, concern, be of support. And he wanted to spend Easter with his son and this time his current wife came along, and when they came out to visit with my son—our son—she and I got a chance to hug and share thoughts about this new journey for the family. Even my ninety-year-old mother has been kind and patient with the situation. These types of things can be transformational, and force you to face the very thing you may have been avoiding. Always be willing to stand in your truth.

3 If I think about what traits I am most proud of, first would be my leadership skills.

These enable me to support people and give back in leading them to a better place and next, would be my integrity. This allows me the ability to stand on what I believe and do what is right, even when the choices may be difficult.

4 Due to my career, being in control and being able to "fix" things has always been a necessary item in my toolbox. And most of the time I am in control, and I have access to the answers to fix things. When I am not, is when I find the most tension in my life. Overall, I have managed things, while keeping aspects of my life on track. For example, when my husband and I divorced after twenty-one years of marriage. We had some very intense moments for the first three to five years, but we were able to get through because I forgave him and understood that our love for our son and grandson was the most important thing. We are still great friends today. Another tense situation was when the theatre that I was working for decided that they wanted to move in a new direction, and they asked me to leave. I had been there for over fifteen years and had sacrificed a lot to stay there. It all became full circle nine years later when they asked me to come back, and I have been back for over fifteen years. Finally, the most dramatic thing in my life occurred when my, at the time twenty-three-year-old son, was sentenced to thirty-five years in prison for an alleged murder charge. That was a nineteen year journey full of anxiety, learning patience, loving unconditionally, and helping your blood find themselves despite the odds against them. Alex Jr. is now home and on parole. The life lessons have been many and continue.

At this stage in my life mid-sixties, I have often felt that Millennials and Gen-Z'ers mistakenly think that being past the age of sixty automatically means our capacity is diminished, and they have an air simply tolerating women like me. I am confident in my training, my professionalism, the accomplishments I have made, and the recognitions I have received as a result of always striving for excellence, therefore my voice will always be preserved.

At the end of the day, I am proud to thank God for granting me the ability to tolerate that which appears different than me, and for providing me with a positive outlook and consideration for others in spite of the challenges I've had to press through. I have found that the beauty of living and learning is that learning never stops until there is no longer a heartbeat. Now I understand that for me wisdom has come with age. I am thankful for knowledge, good judgement that comes from wisdom. Layered in love are the core principles that I received from my mentors and that have sustained me in my life. These principles come from my mother, father, siblings, my early childhood teachers, the life lessons, and my sister friends that have been involved in my life from pre-K to now. For all this I give thanks. EJM

*"The beauty
of a mature woman
is not just
in the lines of her face, but
in the depth of her eyes,
where stories
of courage, love,
and wisdom
reside."*

Dr. ANGELA F. FORD

Executive Vice President,
Black Women's Health Imperative
Upper Marlboro, Maryland

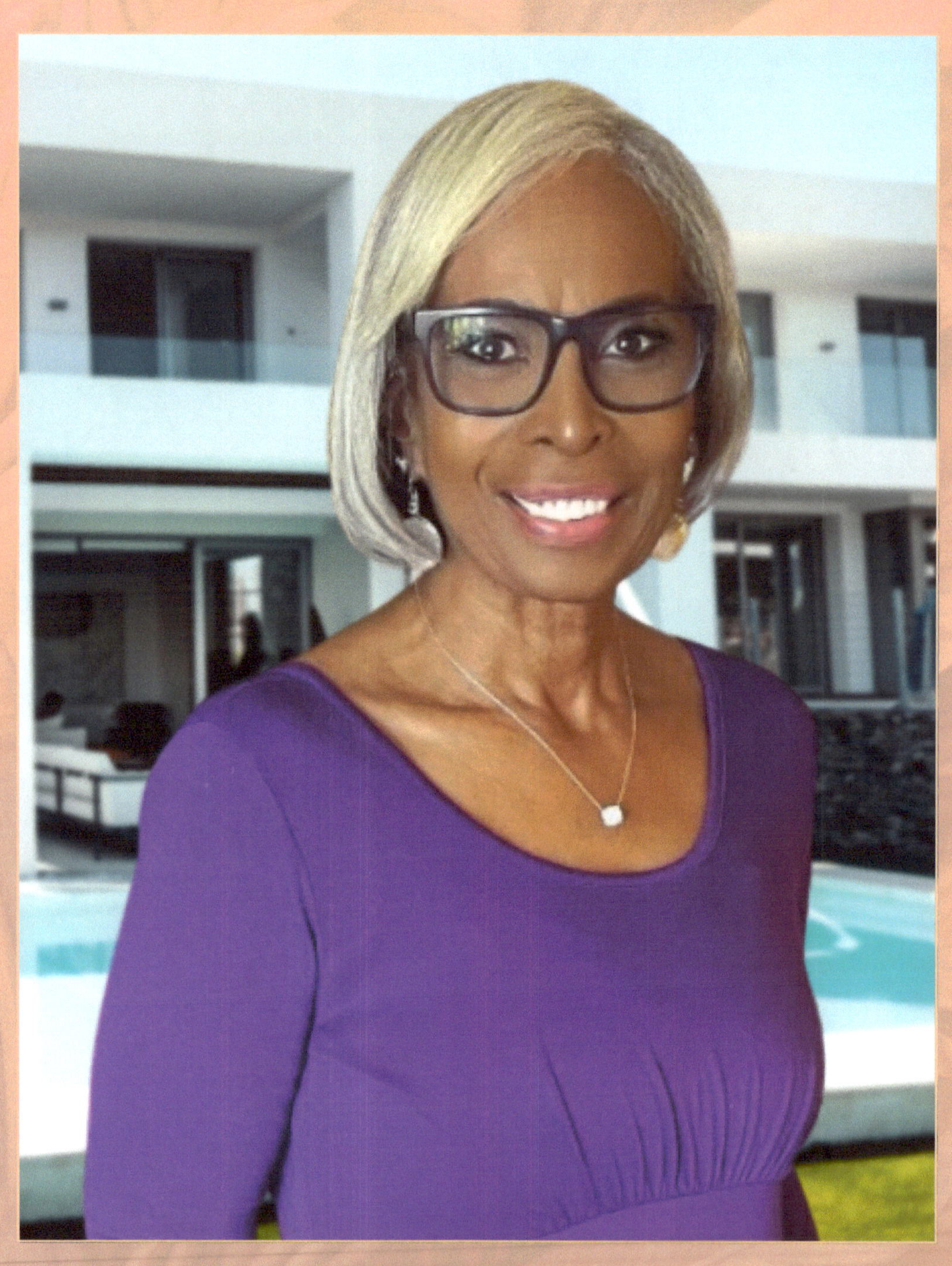

As I write this, I am slowly and most gratefully approaching the seventy-fourth year of my life, which began in Columbus Ohio, where I was born to John and Carrie Graves. I have, rather I had, five older siblings and proudly wore the badge of honor as the baby in the family. Of course, that came with both its blessings and its challenges, and both have been present throughout my life in that role. My childhood was happy and, surrounded by family, and while there was certainly unhappiness around me and what I know now to be generational trauma, I was very much protected from it, or so I thought. I spent much of my childhood living in the same neighborhood with nieces, nephews, and cousins close to my age, so even though my siblings were all seven to fifteen years older, my relatives were like sisters and brothers to me and in fact they were my very first "friends."

When I was in the eighth grade, I became fascinated with my sister's friend's occupation. She was a social work supervisor at the local juvenile detention center. Not sure exactly what the fascination was at that time, but from then on, I knew I wanted to become a social worker. Never wanted to be anything else. However, the school counselor at the high school I was bussed to always discouraged me and attempted to assure me that I should find a job when I finished high school because college was really not for me. But my dad was quite clear that he was taking out a loan and I would be the first in the family to attend college. I recall telling the counselor more than once that my dad says I am going to college even though she insisted that I should not. And attend college, I did! However, I wasn't at all prepared emotionally and almost flunked out the first semester.

My first semester of college was when I met the man, I thought was the love of my life and I guess that was true then, that he was. He was very handsome, four years older than me, and right out of the Air Force. While we didn't date during our freshman year, we ended up together from our sophomore year on. After graduation, we continued to live in separate cities in Ohio and spent as much time together as we could conducting a long-distance relationship. My family loved him and in fact he, in many ways, was a son to my parents who had lost my brother at the age of nineteen. We got engaged and then married about six months after graduation and relocated to Cincinnati, Ohio. Three years later, we were transferred to Los Angeles and as exciting as that was, the same month we got the news about the transfer, we also learned that my father had prostate cancer. While receiving that news all by itself was very heartbreaking, especially since I have always been daddy's girl, I am happy to say that my father survived another twenty-three years.

My first job out of college was during the Model Cities era and it was one of my favorites because I worked with Black women who identified as street workers, offering them the opportunity to participate in a program where they could feel empowered, practice self-care and self-love, attend school, and work as paid interns in their areas of interest. It was such a rewarding experience for me, and I knew then that I really wanted to work with Black women. However, life in Los Angeles included our purchasing a house in the suburbs about twenty-five miles from the city. In the corporate world my husband was a part of, purchasing property meant doing so in an area where it could be sold easily when you were transferred again. As a result, I ended up working as an assistant human resource manager for a poultry processing plant where ninety percent of the employees were Spanish speaking. It was rewarding but experiencing an onsite immigration raid is something I will never forget.

The next relocation was only eighteen months in Indianapolis, Indiana, and we were transferred back to California in Oakland. Now Oakland I loved because about ninety percent of the population was Black, the city was beautiful, close to San Francisco, and I had lots of friends. I worked for the city in the Department of Economic Development and Employment and had the blessing of a supervisor/mentor who introduced me to a strong sense of spirituality, creative visualization, meditation and more. The experience was personally transformative, but my husband began to resent me as he witnessed my evolution. After five years in Oakland, we relocated to Houston, Texas, where I managed a program for Black Vietnam vets to help them find interview for and find jobs. That experience certainly had its extremes. One veteran became quite enraged with me when his post-traumatic stress was triggered, that other veterans had to physically restrain him from attacking me physically. While at the other extreme, another veteran gave me his Captain's bar to show his gratitude for my help, support and his new job.

Pittsburgh is where I spent the next twenty-five years. There, I worked with a head-hunter who focused on my top two choices—counseling and training. While the training position was in corporate America and paid more, I chose the position at Pittsburgh Action Against Rape (PAAR) where I did crisis counseling, legal and medical advocacy, and group counseling with adolescents in group homes and adult women who had been sexually abused as children. I matured so much as a woman in my role at PAAR. I felt like I grew up there. I became very clear in my identity as a Black feminist, I had no doubt in my mind that "choice' is critical in the lives of all women, and I met my best friend in the whole world—Evelyn Savido!

My experience at PAAR was so vast that I could write this entire story about that time of my life. Working with those women shaped my life, my personal beliefs, and my values not only as a woman but also as the mother of two daughters. It grounded me in the values I wanted to pass on to them. That is when I returned to school to work on my Master's degree in social work, ultimately my Doctorate in social work, and a graduate certificate in Gerontology. During my internship at Western Psychiatric Hospital, I not only worked as an in-patient social worker, but I also spent part of the internship at the Alzheimer Disease Research Center (ADRC) and was offered a position as program director responsible for establishing the Alzheimer Outreach Center (AOC) at the Hill House. I absolutely loved that work as well and I have many fond memories of my friend, Bill Blakey, who was the Hill House Superintendent for many years and Audrey Woods, who I hired as a social worker. She and I did great work together.

After four years at AOC, I was asked to consider the position at the new Center for Minority Health in the University of Pittsburgh, Graduate School of Public Health. Like employment in a university setting can be sometimes challenging especially with varying personalities and managing staff, I still found that I loved everything about this experience. It allowed me to continue to work in the community and connect with the heart of my people. I also worked and supervised some wonderful individuals who I remain in love with to this day like Mario Browne, Vicki Garner, Angela Howze, Karen Reddick, Rosie Jones, Felicia Savage, and Chris Howard, who all played a major role in establishing and implementing the Healthy Black Family Project at the Kingsley Association and our health promotion work with local barbershops and hair salons.

Ultimately, I took advantage of an early retirement offer because it was just time to go. I also needed to be physically closer to my own biological family and both daughters were living in other states. However, six months later, I accepted a position with the Black Women's Health Imperative and ten years later, I am still working in what I affectionately refer to as my "retirement job." Currently, as the chief programs officer for the Black Women's Health Imperative, I am in the midst of the most relevant work of my life. Everything about the work, from diabetes prevention to fair work and chronic stress is relevant to my personal existence. Everywhere I go and every Black woman I meet, is connected to my work whether we have a conversation or even know each other or not. The work is about me. The work is about my daughters. The work is about my girlfriends.

So, how do I feel about aging? Not sure how it happened but I became fascinated with older Black women over the years. In fact, my doctoral dissertation was about older Black women and health behavior. I am certain my mother contributed to that. She was poised and graceful and while she struggled with lifelong challenges as a result of her childhood, her pride as a woman was evident. Every day, no matter what was on the schedule, after her bath she adorned herself with her pearl necklace, pearl earrings, her red lipstick, and stockings.

I have always celebrated my age and I have thought of it more as evolving and growing, not about getting old. More like aging like fine wine. The fact is, we didn't get to a certain number and start aging, we have been aging all our lives. While I could focus on the negatives and the challenges throughout my life, I consciously choose not to. Instead, I choose to focus on what was poured into me by other Black women and what I have hopefully poured into them. I have been blessed and will continue to pay those blessings forward. But as AARP wrote in an article a couple of years ago—Ageism is Alive and Well in Advertising! As a result, they began working to disrupt the stereotypes, images, and messaging that we see everywhere. Don't buy into those messages is my advice to younger women who will find themselves walking in the shoes of some older Black woman someday.

I know that is easier said than done but I tend to ignore things that do not represent me, be it gender, race and culture, and age. I assume they are addressing the folks who have the experience represented in the images and messages and not me. Perhaps someday that will be me but at this time in my life it is not. Remember, as Black women, we have a long history of not being portrayed positively in the media, regardless of age. Just do your part to ensure that images and messaging that you use in your work and in your life represent the positive aspects of being whatever age you are. Don't give anyone your power or your joy as a woman, and disrupt, disrupt, disrupt, anything you are faced with that portrays your experience as something you know is not true for you. **AFF**

Dr. LouAnn Ross

Executive Director & President,
Finance of America Cares & Foundation

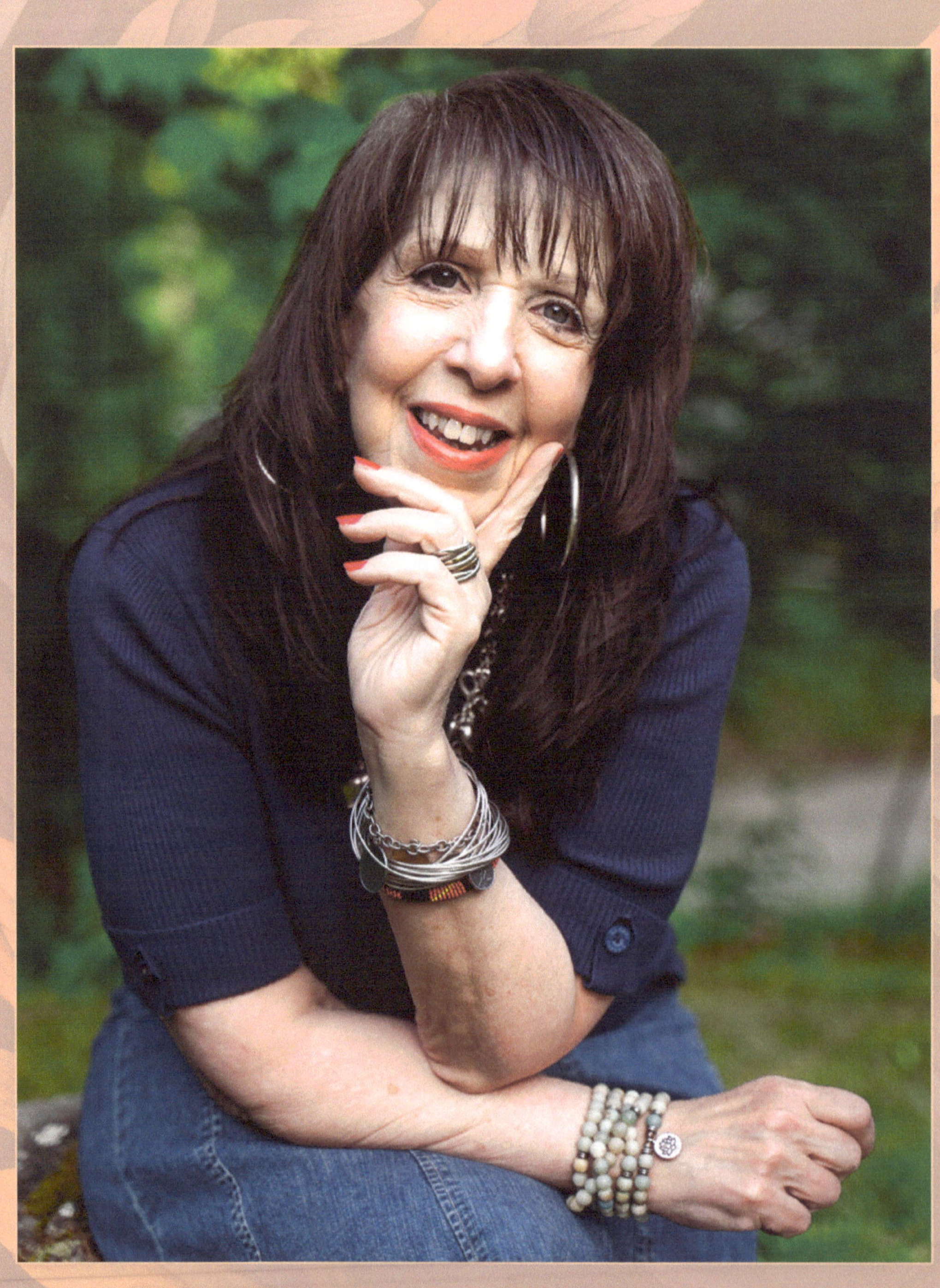

Aging is a curious thing. As I enter my sixty-sixth year, it doesn't' escape me that I have more days behind me than in front of me, and yet most of the time I don't feel much differently than I did in my teens.

My tale is sometimes cautionary, sometimes triumphant and most times just a typical story of a typical woman trying to do her best in those areas that matter most to her. I am honored to share it, because we do not walk this path alone and paving the way for others is an opportunity to walk in grace and provide grace to others in their journey.

Looking over my life, I have had many labels: child, daughter, granddaughter, sister, cousin, niece, Italian American, friend, adult, woman, mother, grandmother (Nonni), domestic violence victim/survivor, wife, student, employee, patient, educator, executive leader, and doctor. I am the granddaughter of Italian immigrants, who grew up in poverty. However, I don't think I knew that since everyone in our circle lived the same experience. We lived in a multi-generational household filled with family and those we thought were family, loud conversations, lots of food, and fortunately for me, strong women with strong opinions and strong voices.

It hasn't been a smooth path or an easy journey, but these experiences have shaped me and led me to the spot where I stand today. I have made many, many bad life decisions over the years, often taking the longest, hardest road to get to a destination. My teen years were filled with examples of those bad choices.

My early twenties began a transitional journey, when I had children, and has lasted my lifetime. Because of them, I was compelled to create a better life and a better world. Before them, I was rudderless. Without them, I am sure I would have remained so. In addition to teaching me the meaning of unconditional love, they taught me that we can accomplish so much more when we are powered by love.

Wanting to create a better life for them gave me the strength to escape domestic violence, push through poverty, homelessness, fear and self-doubt; go back to school while working full-time and running a household; and to strive to be the best version of myself in all things. I often fall short, but I never quit trying.

In my attempt to create a better world for my children, I dedicated my professional self to the nonprofit sector. My path has not been typical. I have worked across numerous sectors to include human services, health care advocacy, community development, public policy, education, and philanthropy. I have gone from cleaning houses in wealthy neigh-borhoods to serving as the CEO of an international organization.

However, long before we heard phrases like the "great resignation" or "quiet quitting," I've had a history of staying in roles for a shorter time than many of my peers. I have changed careers, companies, and titles more than the average person. Mostly, I am restless and curious, but I am also particularly sensitive to professional discomfort with little tolerance for bullying or an unhealthy work culture. Yes, I realize this may be trauma response from my past. Whatever the reason, I haven't typically stayed in any professional role for more than three to five years. While I used to make apologies for this, I don't anymore. I accept this as my truth, even if others don't understand.

I don't imagine ever fully retiring. I want to continue to contribute to making the world a better place and sharing what I've learned. While I am not quite ready to pass the torch completely, I am very determined to share what I have learned with others and clear the path for those coming up behind me. So, while I still serve as a full-time executive, I spend more and more time teaching at the university level, and volunteering and consulting for nonprofit organizations. I imagine that I will be doing more of that in the future.

There are things that are difficult about growing older; losing loved ones at a seemingly more rapid pace, aches and pains that grow exponentially, constantly misplacing the car keys or cell phone, but there are so many wonderful things as well. I have learned to accept those things about myself that don't necessarily make sense to others. As long as I am not hurting anyone else, I don't apologize for my life choices. I find myself more accepting of others as well—meeting them wherever they are. If, for some reason I can't, I harbor no ill will. While I've lost some of my physical balance, I've gained greater emotional balance.

I also find that the older I get, the less material things mean to me. I strive to have and share experiences with others instead. My father passed away when he was only forty-eight years old, and I often think about all of the things he missed. It wasn't what he would have earned or bought, but the birth of his grandchildren, marriages, graduations, holiday gatherings, family vacations, laughter, and love and more. Those are the things that he missed. On my more reflective days, I think about all of the things I have experienced since my forty-eighth year, and I am overwhelmed by each day, each experience, and by the opportunity to grow older.

Being a woman has its own challenges, aging as a woman, even more so. Expectations for women are complex, and just when I think I've learned them, they change. Pre-conceived notions about women of a certain age can be limiting. That is frustrating as I don't see myself any differently, as a matter of fact, I feel I have more to offer, not less. I no longer speak for approval, but instead remain focused on my goals, my mission and my values. My once well-intentioned but some time reckless urgency, has been replaced with thoughtful and intentional movement. Now I more readily admit my mistakes and take time when making decisions. Others often see these as weaknesses, but they are adjustments as a result of life's lessons, and not because of what is perceived as diminished energy ability or engagement.

SEASONS

Life can come fast and furious. One moment, life can be as simple as sorting your laundry without a care and the next you find yourself navigating some truly traumatic events. Age and experience teach us how quickly things can change and much has changed for me over the years. I have gone from homelessness to living quite comfortably, from wild and temperamental to calm and accepting, from poverty to financial security. But there is never a time that I forget my journey, where I have been and what I had to do to get here. Other people, smarter and more hard working than I, have not had my good fortune and I remain keenly aware of and humbled by this.

My life has been a series of miracles. I have survived to this point, often despite myself. My path hasn't been without its turns, detours, and tumbles, and yet I have few regrets. For good or for bad, I've learned from every experience. Although I am not sure as to why the lessons are strongest when times have been the hardest, I have had the opportunity to love deeply and experience joy to my core. I wouldn't trade that for anything, including a wrinkle-free face or the skip in one's step that is reserved for only the young.

Three things I know for sure … I think?
1. Stay grateful, see everything single thing as the Miracle it is.
2. Don't give up, you'll figure it out. You really will.
3. Love is always, always, always the answer. LAR

"With each
passing year,
a mature woman
doesn't age; she evolves,
becoming a
more refined version
of herself, confident in her
journey and her place
in the world."

GERALDINE MASSEY

Community Family Support Therapist
Center for Victims of Violence & Crime
Pittsburgh, Pennsylvania

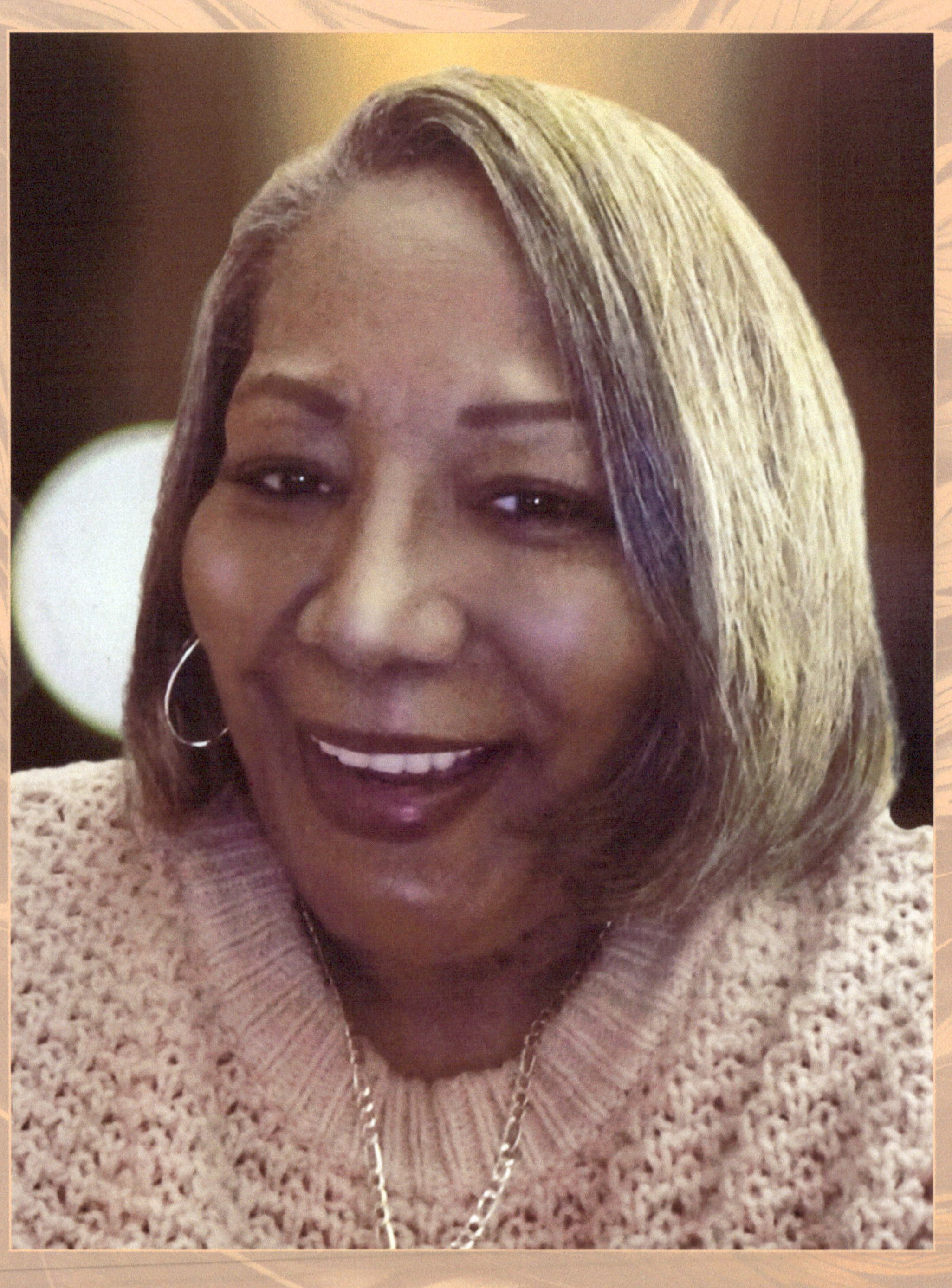

Maintaning Relevancy
in the Seasoned Years

I am amazed at how alive and full of life I feel. I have been on a journey that could have only been planned by God. When anyone greets me and asks, "How are you doing today," I reply, "I am blessed and highly favored." I say this and mean it from the bottom of my heart.

I was born in Pittsburgh to my parents Gerald and Jean West. I am the middle child of five children and the oldest of my father's children. My parents taught us to give service to our family and community. I am grateful for all the redirection I received from my parents and extended family. I am the mother of five children, three living—Kelly, Amber, Ebony, and two deceased—Omar and Gerald.

In 1993, I lost my husband to colon cancer. On October 3rd, my youngest son, Gerald, was murdered sitting on a porch in Hazelwood during a party. Then a month later, on November 8th, my second son, Omar, was also killed during a home invasion.

My older two sisters both died from cancer, neither of them lived to be fifty years old. I did not realize the effect this had on my life until my 50th birthday was approaching fast, and thank God I was healthy that I began to look at my life through a different lens.

I spent twelve wonderful days in Jamaica in my 50th year, number four on my bucket list then. I went back to school full-time to get my bachelor's degree. I graduated with my Bachelor of Science from Carlow University in 2010 when I was fifty-six years young. I could not believe it; I had a college degree and how proud my parents would have been. How proud was I, wow, like a room without a roof.

It was then that I realized that I had not only experienced my 50th birthday, but I had also earned a degree while maintaining a full-time job. What a life I have. I am so grateful for the entire journey to this point. I was drawn to a Graduate Program for Professional Counseling and decided to apply for admission.

I received my Master of Science degree in 2014 at the age of sixty-two. I was feeling like I was limitless. I had now lived twelve years longer than my older siblings. I was healthy, blessed, and highly favored.

I bought my first home the next year in 2015 and began practicing as a therapist. On January 24, 2023, I became a licensed professional counselor by the State of Pennsylvania at the young age of seventy-one years of age. I am a living example that you cannot count us golden seasoned women out when it comes to being goal oriented and focused on living our best life. I am proud of my age and grateful for all my accomplishments in my life.

I received my wisdom from the elder women in my village and those that I saw who carried themselves with pride and dignity. I also received wisdom from my father, he made sure that I would become a well-rounded woman.

My grandmother was the major source for my spiritual influence and a major contributor to my sense of self. She taught me how to love myself like God does.

I have always tried to make significant contributions to my work as well as my community. I have always been a person who loves to provide help to others. I was raised to help those that are not as fortunate as I am. I volunteer my time whenever and wherever I can do so. Helping others rejuvenates my spirit and lights up my life.

When I get a chance to speak to young women, I make sure I tell them that they have the power to be and do whatever they want to do, and when they do it is not relevant as the fact that they did it. I would tell them they have the responsibility to teach young men and women how to respect, love, honor and promote themselves through any of life's difficulties. They will at some time become the elders of the community and how they live; their life is always being observed and disseminated by the young people around them.

Being able to record my successes, accomplishments, and blessings of my golden years is a privilege and I feel honored to be a part of this project. I pray that someone who gets this information is made better because of it, or at the very least come to realize that no matter what they face, they are not alone, and that there is always light on the other side, and there is recovery, and that no matter what—THINGS DO GET BETTER. GM

SHARON GREENE

Retired, Salon Owner

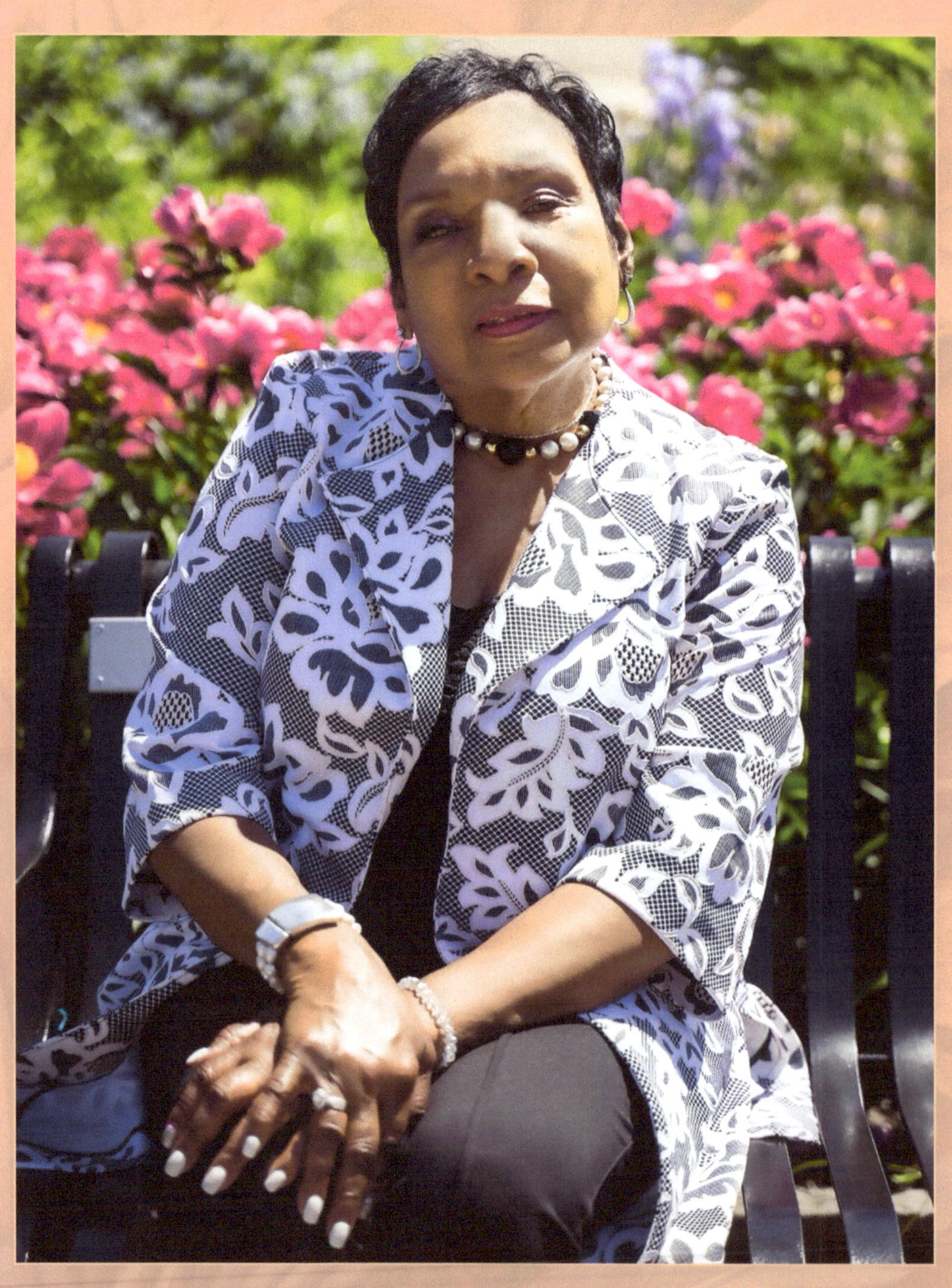

A Kept Woman

I'm sure you're looking at the title wondering what it means, but as I go through this snapshot of my journey, it will be clear.

My name is Sharon Tipton Greene (Tipton is my mom's family name). I am the ripe, but young age of seventy-three, lol. I am a part of a family that consisted of ten children, seven boys and three girls. This was okay for my mother, because she came from a family of twelve and they were made up of eight girls, and four boys. You can imagine during this time life was not easy financially for families—especially ones with so many children. Although my grandfather who was an entrepreneur, he did much to aide in providing for us when alive.

He died too young, and I was too young to glean knowledge from him. Knowledge that could have taught and inspired as I embarked on my road to self-sufficiency at an earlier age. However, I am convinced that being an entrepreneur is in my DNA, came from my grandfather whom I affectionately called "Poppa." The stories of how hard he worked to be independent where amazing.

During the early years of my life, maybe until the age of eleven or twelve, my mother was a single parent. We didn't have a lot in terms of material possessions, we were by most standards poor but we were rich in ways some folks never got to experience.

Through love, family bonds, spiritual connections, and the absolute presence of respect for those who made up our village. Through this, I learned to persevere, and later learned to thrive.

Unfortunately, I also learned to mask a lot of secret traumas, out of shame, that didn't break me, but gave me a strength that I should not have possessed at such an early age.

My love for going to church, singing in the choir, vacation bible school was the perfect outlet in a community that was pretty isolated. It definitely aided in building my character and establishing my value system. But it also later gave me a clear reality that God allows things to happen, good and bad, and it doesn't mean he has abandoned me.

So fast forward, I married and had two handsome sons. Unfortunately, my marriage did not last—I had certain expectations and they were not lived up to. Quickly I had to think of something that would sustain myself and my children. I abandoned the idea of going to college, which oftentimes I regretted, and enrolled in Pittsburgh Beauty Academy. I knew I needed to provide for myself and my children quickly.

Hair-styling was a gift that I already had, but I was never really interested in pursuing the craft, but once I embarked upon the career, I learned to love it, and it sustained me over the last forty plus years.

This career has allowed me to be more than just a business owner, but an employer, friend, family therapist, confidant, and more because interacting with people we become invested in them, they believe in us, they put a lot of trust in what we do, and what we think, our opinion matters, and I don't take that for granted. Whatever I do I try to do it as unto God.

Whether we know it or not, wherever we go we are taking our pulpit, if you will, with us. If we're believers, this understanding is paramount for our lives. Our jobs and our careers are our gifting, it is also our ministry, and we should do them as unto God.

I could have done somethings differently that could have enhanced my career. But

I'm convinced that we go through what we go through because there is something that we need to learn from it all and there's no getting around it.

As far as my personal life journey goes, I've only been married once. I've always dreamed of having the house with the white picket fence. But for some reason that did not happen. I am not sure if it was because of something I did or did not do. Or if the opportunity came to me and I wasn't paying attention and therefore missed it. Or perhaps that scenario was not supposed to be in the cards for me.

I've had several relationships but none of them evolved to what is most important to me—the unity and sanctity of marriage. I desired a successful marriage as a young woman, and I still desire it as a woman in my senior years. I do believe that we were not created to be alone.

One of the pitfalls, I believe, happens to women who consider themselves to be independent, is that they give off the aura to men that they're not approachable. Their strength sometimes sends a message—misinterpreted—that they don't need anyone.

Many times, a woman inside may be screaming, "Pick me…pick me lol." I'm chuckling but at least I know I've felt this way. So, I think that we as women need to be mindful of the fact that we can be, and should be strong, but we're not an island, we don't need to do it all ourselves. It can be a hinderance, and deterrent to meeting and attracting "Mr. Right."

I mean that's basically one of the lying things that I was taught—*don't let a man do something for you, YOU can do for yourself*—had me patching my front steps up every summer because the cement would crack, instead of asking for help. Really?! God created men to be our help mates Just as he created us to be theirs. Submission does not equate to passiveness, it is so misconstrued.

I know that for me rejection has been one of the things that has kept me from being as open as I could have been. All these things left me feeling rejected.

Divorce = Rejection

Failed relationships = Rejection

Broken promises = Rejection

Also being violated sexually as a young child can leave scars and deep-rooted problems that must be dealt with. Many times, as women we don't work through the things that have happened to us; we try to present like we are so strong that we can just get over things. What happens when we do not get help for our trauma, it impacts us in many negative ways. It also dictates how we interact with people, causing us to shut down to friendships and new relationships. And we do not understand where our attitudes are coming from. It is because we have not done the work nor have we worked on our healing.

I've learned to push through my challenges and at the same time realize that my life is not my own that I'm not operating through this life by flesh and blood, because I'm spirit and created in God's image. I do understand that I will continue to face difficult days, and challenges, but I know that just like in the past, my faith will help me get through.

I've always held on to the promises of God, I focus on the blessings I've experienced and not the mishaps. I feel that if it were not for my faith, and my belief that no matter what God will keep me, I would be in bad shape—but I am not, because of His grace and mercy, and that is everything to me.

When I've had a diagnosis that was not positive, and yes, I've had a few, I can't say that I didn't cry, but once the crying was over, I shook myself off, and planted my feet firmly knowing that the only way I could move through it was if I remained steady and believed that I could move through it.

I could not approach it from the bottom I had to approach it from the top. I had to see myself already threw it, it's the only way I could deal with it. In 2010, in a three-month time period, doctors found a mass on my brain, I was diagnosed with thyroid cancer and spinal stenosis.

So, if I had to give advice to a younger woman the first thing I would say is have faith. That is the most important foundation you can have. Ask God for His advice. Consult His plans for your life. Surround yourself with like-minded people, think of yourself as an eagle. Everything they do is at an advantage because they position themselves at a high vantage point, they are observing, planning, waiting, and implementing at just the right time.

Believe in yourself and know there's nothing that you cannot achieve. Write your vision and put it in front of you. Know where you want to go and start working towards it. Plan, plan, plan! Not planning was a pitfall for me; I've learned!

Don't let anyone tell you what you cannot do. You have the ability to create wealth. We all have a gift inside of us so find out what that gift is. It will be the only thing that's going to make you happy, anything else you do is going to be work, but when you work in your gifting, your natural ability, you will have pleasure each of your working days.

Although things may shake you because life is not always steady, know that you can start over if you need to. Don't be hard on yourself, and certainly don't allow others to beat you up. You are a viable part of this fabric called life and your contribution is important.

This might make you chuckle, as I am now when I write this, but this stage of life there are things I still desire, particularly a husband and thus companionship. Although I've learned how to be comfortable in my singleness. But more than anything I've learned that joy, peace, and happiness far surpasses any connection that's not happy, and material things surely wear out. I would like to believe that I have left some nuggets along the way, and I've surely received some.

If I could adjust one thing in my life, I would have loved on myself a lot more, not diminishing any love I've shown to others: but remembering my worth at the same time.

Remember, I titled this *A Kept Woman*, well that was not from a man, but by God "El Roi" which means the God that sees me! He has kept me through it all. **SG**

He knows my name!

PATRICIA ARMSTEAD DANIELS

Retired, OR Nurse
Pittsburgh, Pennsylvania

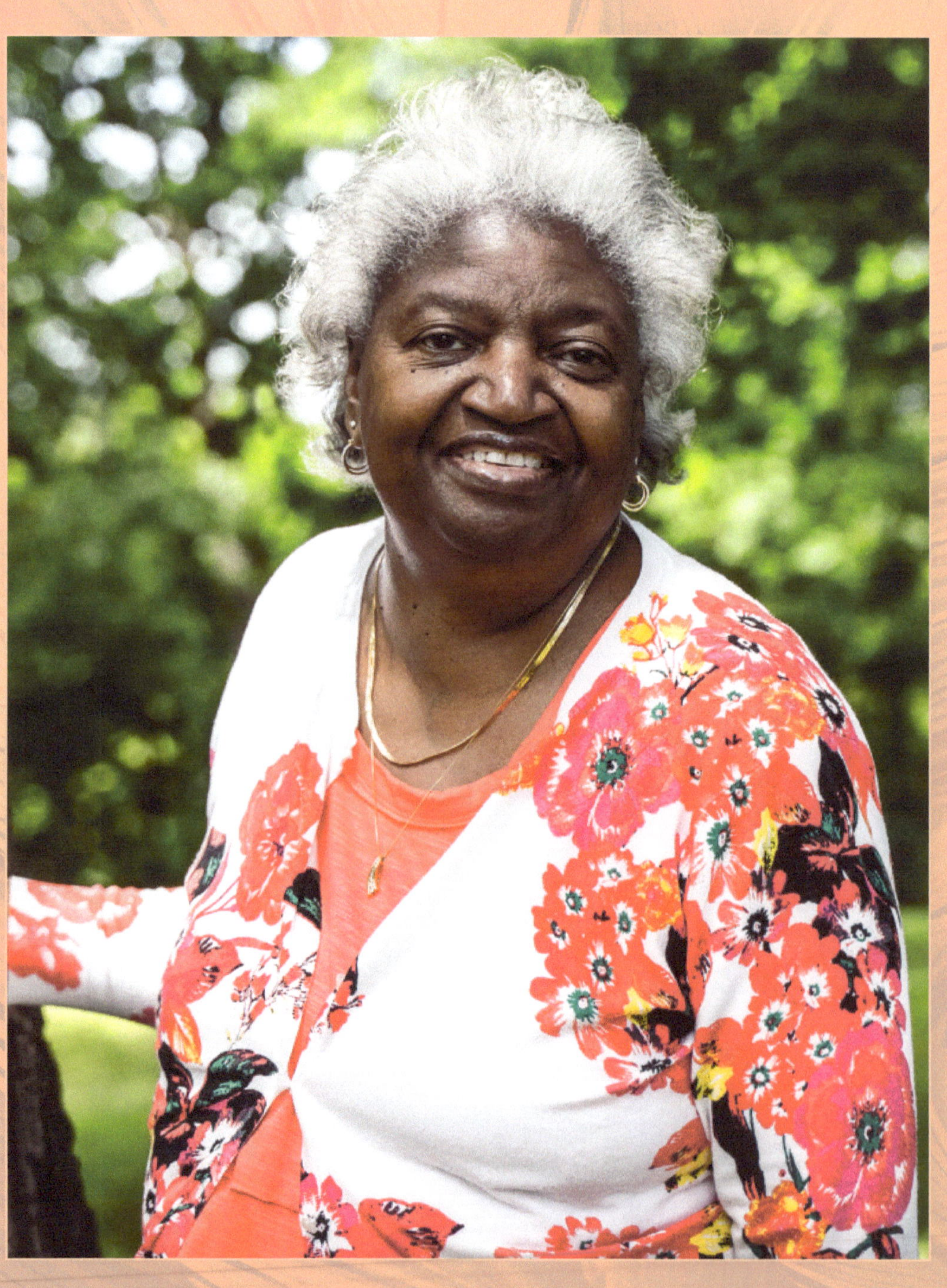

The Perfect Way to Age Learn, Grow, Expand, Be Open— *Then Repeat the Process*

I was born August 26, 1950, the second eldest child of a single mother—I had four siblings. Life was not easy in the 1950's for a young woman with five children out of wedlock. However, my mom was smart, resourceful and strong. She never missed an opportunity to teach us life lessons. Those lessons were not always easy to hear, but they prepared us for the struggles that were sure to come.

Education was extremely important in our household. You could often find us all sitting around the kitchen table doing our homework. We were taught from a very young age that nothing was beyond our reach if we studied and worked towards it.

Like many young women from my era, I dreamed of an exciting career, which included travel and meeting people from all walks of life. However, I was steered towards those professions that were acceptable for a young Black woman—a nurse or a teacher.

I chose nursing. I finished my nursing program after I was married with one child.

My husband was very supportive until I completed my studies. He did not want his wife to work. One of the life lessons that my mom taught me was that I should always strive to keep the peace in my home. So, we came to an agreement, and I waited until our daughter went to full-time kindergarten.

If you have ever been the only one or one of a few African Americans in any environment, you know that it was no walk in the park. Everything you did or said was under constant scrutiny. We had to always be the best and work the hardest. In many instances we were paid much less than our white counterparts, male and female. When I look back over my life, I wonder how I was able to succeed and prosper.

For years, I worked at nursing jobs that were not what I wanted. I learned a lot and met many interesting individuals, but I was still not satisfied. I wanted to be an operating room nurse, but that job in Pittsburgh was not one that Black nurses were even considered for least of all hired. In fact, I had to leave the state to get the job that I wanted.

I had been hired as a floor nurse at the University of Virginia Medical Center and was waiting in the nursing office to take a tour of my new unit. While waiting, I overheard an administrator trying to convince another new hire to consider employment in the operating room. The nurse apologized and said that was not a position she was wanted. I walked over to the woman and shared my lifelong desire to work in the operating room. And so, it was.

Working in the operating room was exciting and stressful. Surgical nursing then was not as specialized as it is currently. We were required to learn just about every service, scrubbing and circulating. The surgeons treated us with respect, and we were valued members of the surgical team.

As we all know, nothing ever stays the same, this was true for the nursing profession as well. Many nurses were choosing travel nursing, for employment. It was an opportunity to choose when, where and how long you wanted to work at any given facility.

I was an Operating Room (OR) nurse for thirty years. I had to move my family to Charlottesville, Virginia to get the job paying the dollars I knew I was worth.

I learned a great deal from this work. One of the things that stands out the most was the humility that was brought to bear. I recall how God allowed surgeons to pull people through, and how different they were from when they arrived—it was overwhelming at best. But to realize you were just a small piece of that picture, but you still had a roll in serious healing was humbling.

For me, the takeaway from experiencing this environment every day, is that no matter what you know or how good you are at any job, there is always something to know that can make you better. Even as I have aged, I am experiencing something new if I can. The thing is to incorporate those things to your life to make it better.

What I would leave to younger women: being open is what keeps us relevant. Open to new things, and continued learning. When we stop doing that, or when we shut down from that, is when we lose our relevancy.

What I've come to recognize through the aging process is that there is value in staying open and there is always something to learn. My mother was an incredible example of what it meant to keep on learning. She had a couple professions while she was raising us. She was a cook at a private school for years, who ultimately became the kitchen manager, and as such oversaw hiring and training of new staff. In order to do that she had to go through a food service training program and had to go through the food safety certification program through the Allegheny County Department of Health. Additionally, she completed beauty school, and became a licensed beautician, and ran a business out of our home. It is safe to say that she simultaneously conducted these two professions over the entire period of raising us and retiring.

Watching her gave me the bird's eye view of what it was to work and learn and grow and keep doing all of the above in order to sustain oneself and one's family. She had a very calm spirit within all of this and that spilled over into all of this. That trait would serve me well as my own life continued to develop and I would experience things that would render anyone without a smooth spirit completely off their level footing.

Overall, due to my mother and grandmother's influence in my life I was blessed to be able to witness wisdom being played out in its truest form, and I was also able to acquire and cultivate that same wisdom and use it to my good. What I learned from them helped me to navigate through some of life's most sudden and trying times.

SEASONS

Since none of us can predict the future, I learned that we should always be ready. So, when I lost my husband, and my mother in the same year—within months of each other, I was thrown for a loop. It took all I had to keep standing and to still see a future for myself. Essentially, I was a very young widow with a daughter, and I had to totally revamp myself.

But I found the strength to carry own. And keep moving forward. I was already an OR nurse and was able to manage financially. Even though I discovered my husband owed some back taxes from significant lottery winnings that I had not been informed of, and there was an issue with our car insurance and the insurance company was giving me a hard time about paying. You see my husband lost his life due to a car accident and the car had not been paid for. I was faced with what seemed like insurmountable obstacles, but I had my mother and grandmother's DNA, and defeat was not an option.

I would ultimately remarry and once again relocated back to Charlottesville. Several years later, when my beautiful, brilliant, funny, talented adult daughter, who was living her best life, working for a major corporation living in Reston, VA, doing amazing well with her life died after a surgery—when I truly felt defeat sweep over me, when my knees buckled threating my very ability to exist—even then, I knew I had to carry on.

If I wasn't for the strength of my faith, losing my only child could have collapsed me. In spite of it though, that loss, the others, and subsequent more, what I have found is that God has not abandon me. I am now retired from nursing. I have returned to Pittsburgh and I find that my interests continue to expand. I have always been a very good cook. And food service is a major contribution to any endeavor. Additionally, I never shied away from technology, so I recently begun taking computer classes. And am involved in the work my church does in my community.

I encourage any one of you young women whose future awaits you. When you have the opportunity to be more, to do just that, become all that you can by adopting three agreements with yourself: **1)** Keep learning and work on multiple streams of income if you can even though advancing oneself isn't always about money. **2)** Be open to the good things about life and people as this will get you through the gray places and midnight moments that are sure to come. **3)** Lastly, understand that giving back is a blessing within itself. God

*"The world
may change,
but the essence
of a mature woman
remains: a beacon of
grace, strength, and
unwavering spirit,
proving that
true confidence
is ageless."*

TERRI LYNN SHIELDS

Founder and Executive Director, Jada House International

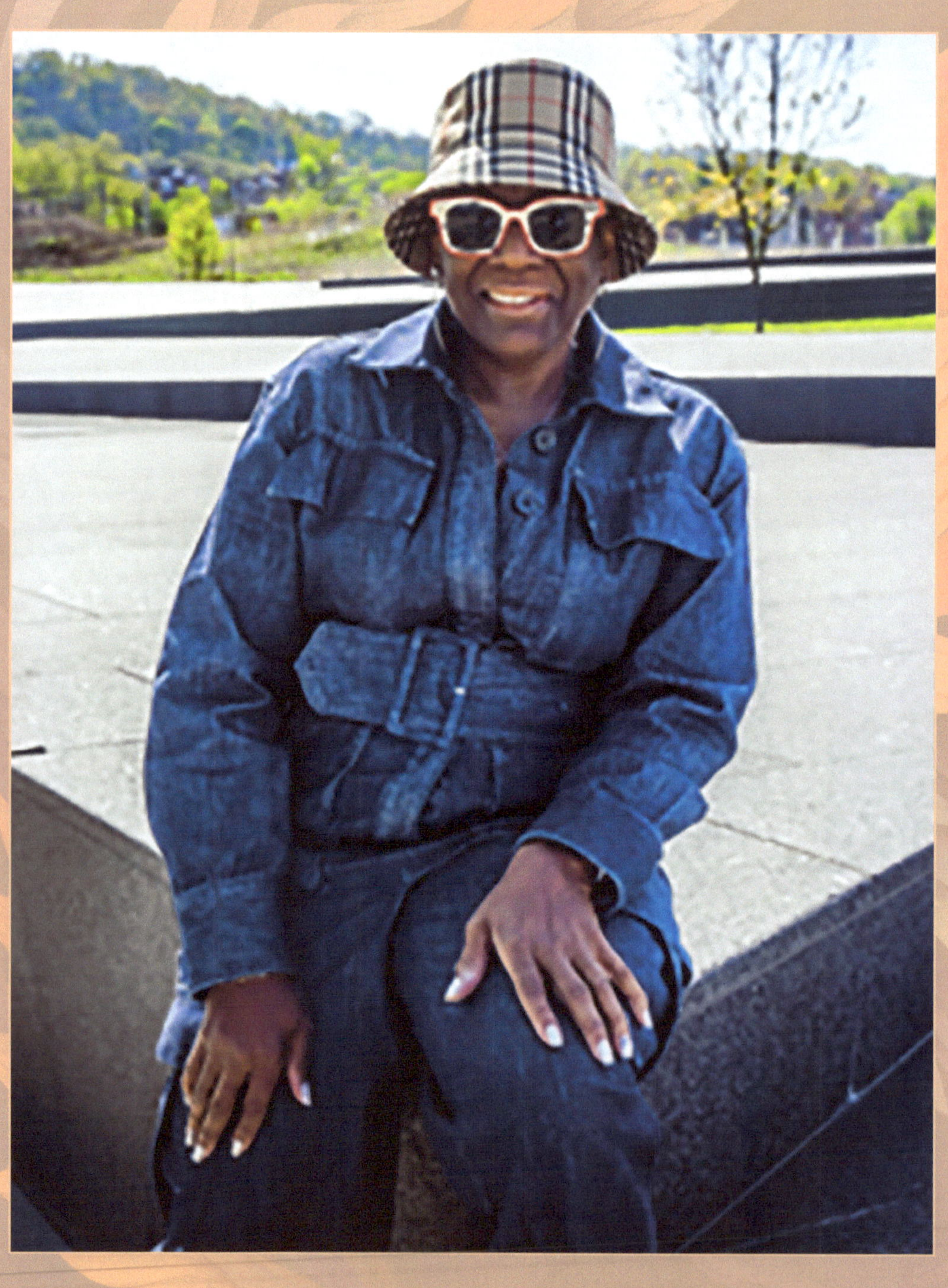

"Though thy beginning was small, yet thy latter end should greatly increase." —Job 8:7

Terri Lynne Shields, here, I'm sixty-three years of age. I am the Founder and Executive Director of JADA House International, a nonprofit for nine years. I recently retired from UPMC Health Plan, where I was a workforce supervisor for twenty-two years. The above scripture is a most accurate description of the journey of my life.

For the nine years of the existence of JADA House, I was also working full time. The efforts of JADA House, included putting together a board, holding meetings, planning for each session, and running the non-profit in general. It became too much. I had no idea when I started JADA House that it would evolve and become all that it has. It soon became pretty clear that in stepping back and forth between the two, that I was not fulfilling my purpose.

I grew up in Hazelwood, Pennsylvania, Glen Hazel to be exact. For the first nine years of my life, I was an only child. Mine was a two-parent household and my mother worked for the county, and my stepdad worked in the steel mill. Mom was the disciplinarian in the family, and my stepdad was responsible for most of the financials. Summers were spent in Opa-locka, Florida. Visiting my grandmother, I didn't necessarily appreciate the value of these trips at the time because of my youth, but I did like the part where we went to downtown Miami to shop, as well as going to Miami Beach after church on Sundays. After these two things, I was always ready to return home, but that wasn't to be—I was on vacation.

By the time I was seventeen years of age, I had my first child. At the age of twenty-four, I had three children. As I think back, I see that single moms don't always understand what the effects of their decisions—good and bad—have on our children. However, I did what I needed to do to provide for my children and myself. My head was in a lot of places at that time, I was attempting to be independent, which meant taking care of us, trying to be a mother my children while at the same time trying to hold on to a piece of my own childhood which I didn't realize was gone forever. Consequently, I made some poor judgement calls, resulting in poor choices—resulting in negative consequences.

My unfortunate decisions ultimately sent me down a path that led to shame for my mom, my children, and myself. Regrettably it would take multiple arrests and a debt paid to society to wake me up—I had to get my life together. That journey began by me securing a job with Allegheny County as a cook at John J. Kane Regional Center that was a senior nursing home. Within a year's time I went from part-time to full-time, which came with full benefits. I saw this as a blessing and considered myself as such! Especially since I was still facing the results of some of those bad choices and had a court hearing coming up that would determine my fate for the crimes I had committed.

Even though I was making strides to establish a better life for me and my children, and I had turned from my "street ways," my self-esteem had tanked. I had not learned how to forgive myself for my mistakes, and bad judgement so, I had a head filled with negative thoughts. I convinced myself that my changes did not matter and that it was too little, too late. I was sure I was stuck in the job at Kane. The voices stayed in my head, telling me things like I was not smart enough to return to school, so maybe I should just settle for being a cook for the rest of my life. And that the hearing was going to result in worse outcome possible which would be that I'd get carried off to jail for an extended time. Well God is the orchestrator of our lives, I only ended up getting probation—and not only was I smart enough for school, but I have also gone back to school, got my Bachelor's degree, and am currently working on my Master's—praise God indeed. My latter is better than my former.

When I went into the court room, I believe the judge saw my commitment to change, because I had not one job, but two, part-time jobs. He most likely saw potential in me and determined that jail time would not serve me as much as being able to continue to turn my life around would. And consequently, placed me on seven years' probation.

With that behind me, I was now free to focus on next steps for the plan for my life. I began to think about going back to school for social work. I always wanted to help people from the time I lived in the Hill District as I was always there for my neighbors. I fed folks in my court, often welcomed people to stay at my home for a short period of time and, essentially, was always willing to try and help wherever I could. I lived on Hill, about seven years before I decided to move my family back home to Hazelwood.

I and my three children moved to 718 Johnston Ave, the same house my sister and I grew up in. It is the same house I left at age nineteen to explore my "grownness" and I now had gone full circle and moved back. My sister and my mom had moved out of that same house to take residence outside of the Hazelwood community. In the meantime, I continued work at Kane hospital. I went from dietary aid to a cook. I was a pretty good worker and things were going well, but as I watched the older women around me with various ailments, I decided that would not be me, and I would not be there for the rest of my life.

I registered with Community College of Allegheny County. (CCAC) At the time of registration, I was still only working part time, I figured I could do both—work part time and go to school in the evening. However, that would not be because I learned the same day of registration that I had been moved from part-time dietary aide to a full-time cook. I would have to change my schedule from a daytime student to part time, going a few nights a week.

Raising three kids single handily was not easy. And there were things I didn't get completely right because I was in survival mode. My focus was school, work, and making sure bills were paid. Making sure my kids went to school and were dressed appropriately.

In the meantime, my vision for my family got bigger as I was tired of housing projects. I set my sights on purchasing a house. My job at Kane Hospital would put that goal within my reach among other things, like a car, and new furniture.

I was thrilled that I begin to see my capacity getting stronger. I was thirty-three years old and I had completed the program at CCAC and now had my associate degree, I was a homeowner and had got my first car. Again, my latter was looking better than my former.

It gave me the courage I needed to make a professional move, and that was to quit the cook's job. My mom was worried, "Terri Lynne are you sure want to do this? After all you have those good benefits ... maybe you should think about it."

"Mom, I will think about it, but I know I am not staying in this job for the benefits. I just don't want to look up 20 years from now and find myself a senior citizen in this job, still in the kitchen cooking."

I begin looking around applying for jobs. I was always taught "we don't leave a job until we found another one." Even though my old negative thoughts resurfaced, "reassuring" me that my background would keep me from getting hired—I still trusted that God would help me, I literally stepped out on faith and applied for a job with one of the city's major health plans—UPMC. Once in their human resource department, in Oakland, my ragged nerves kicked in fully. And they really begin to rage as the interview began. All was good until we got to that famous question asked, "Have you ever been convicted of a crime/felony?" I answered honestly, "Yes, I was convicted of retail theft, which resulted in a felony charge." She wrote something down on my résumé or my application. After the interview, I left that building thinking, "Well I guess I won't get that job ... they're not going to hire me." At the end of one week, I was at work when I got the phone call. She said, "Is this Terri Shields? I have a job for you at UPMC and Western Psychiatric Institute & Clinic (WPIC) the John Merk Residential Treatment Facility (RFT) working with children."

I was excited beyond measure and was walking on air a bit. My duties would include administering tuberculosis as well as drug tests. This change not only took me out of the kitchen at Kane Hospital but was far more than I expected. "Now to him who is able to do immeasurably more than all we ask or imagine, according to his power that is at work within us." Ephesians 3:20 (NIV)

Moving to my new job showed me I had broken what I deemed to be an impenetrable barrier for myself and my background was no longer a threat to me. And this was just the beginning of me pushing past my past. The new job did pay less money, however, so I had to secure a second job but hard work did not frighten me. The second job would be at Family Links. I recall the interview and being asked the same question. This time I had a different response—it was bolder, and I was more self-assured. That is what time and experience does for you—makes you more self-assured. When asked what my crime was, I confidently replied, "I paid my debt to society, are you going to hire me or not?" I was hired on the spot. I was now a teacher counselor at Family Links in the evening, working at a residential treatment facility in the daytime.

As time passed it was clear that my associate degree was not going to be enough. I entered Carlow University to get my bachelor's degree in Communications. At the same time my career was continuing to take hold, working two jobs, and raising my family. I transferred a few times within UPMC. While at WPIC I actually received an award — ACES (Award for Commitment and Excellence in Service) this was for employees who did outstanding work. At WIPC, I worked first with children experiencing mental health issues, then dual diagnosis rehab. I would end my career with UPMC, working for the health plan.

In the meantime, my personal life was getting turned upside down. As I was preparing myself to provide a better life for my future and my children—I became a grandmother at the age thirty-four. I was not ready for that as I recall the anger and confusion I felt, as I wondered, just what was I going to do now? Here I was a grandmother and mother taking care of everyone in the household. Then living in a community where everyone knows you, is connected by either love or blood or the street you lived on, there was that embarrassment and a little bit of family shame that had to be managed. By God's grace we got through it and once my grandson was born, I fell in love, he was my world.

One night in 2008, health issues visited me. I was awakened with excruciating pain in my right wrist. It was so bad I had to go to the ER that night. They took blood and gave me medicine to cause the inflammation to go down. I was good after that as months went by without any serious problems. However, again one early morning, I woke to severe pain throughout my body. I later learned I was in Lupus crisis and the pain was so bad that just the touch of a sheet being placed on my skin was painful.

I went back to the emergency room, they took blood again, gave me an IV of prednisone, and I started to feel better. They prescribed me a high dose prednisone and sent me home. A couple weeks later I got a phone call at work, with a nurse telling me I had Lupus. All I could think about is a childhood friend who died from Lupus. I called my mother in hysterics as fear had overtaken me and all I could think of was I was going to die. My mother told me to calm down.

I couldn't figure out why this nurse who called me would tell me something like that on the phone and it was very insensitive and made no sense to me. And for a bit I was getting the run around until my manager who was a nurse herself referred me to the Lupus Center of Excellence. They did extensive blood work, and a bone density test. They even experimented with what medication I should be on.

In the meantime, I was in denial about all of this, and would often stop taking the medicine whenever I felt good. A mix of vanity and carelessness almost cost me my life. I thought I was too cute to have some type of damn autoimmune disease. I played with my medicine, but I just played myself. In 2012, my kidneys shut down first, though I recovered from that, but it was followed up with congestive heart failure. I was in a comatose state. As my mom prepared to come visit me, she shared that God prepared her by saying to her, "Do not believe what you are about to see." I was literally on my death bed. I was in ICU for at least five days, my mother was praying for me around the clock, and I was in a state of not knowing what's going on. And I feel left over tears as I write about it at this at this moment—passed sixty—God delivered me because he had something in mind for me. My latter was definitely going to be better than my former.

During my life changing experience with my health, I decided—well God gave me a second chance— to totally redirected my life. The Bible tells us He knew us before we were in our mother's wombs, and He knew what He had set out for me. So, it was beyond time to get my spirit intact, I wanted to have a closer relationship with God. It was time to find out why I was still here, what purpose did He have for me. I was encouraged to become a deaconess in my church. I went to classes and was taught the duties of a deaconess and I love being connected with Him.

Our church had or was starting a women's ministry. After attending a few of the sessions, it occurred to me that women needed a place where they could be more transparent in a place, they felt safe to do so. Many times, women do not find this safety in the church environment, as much as it would seem so. I knew this because personally I had a lot going on, my beloved grandson was incarcerated, I was raising his sisters, my granddaughters, and while I was blessed to have help from my mother and my aunt, I was still doing a lot like working two jobs and going to school and still try to party a little, on whatever level I could.

My vision for JADA HOUSE, became clearer, and I went to my bishop to present the vision God gave me. However, God has perfect timing, and that was not good timing for the vision to be in collaboration with my church. Still, I was obedient, and my vision carried and JADA House International came into being. Its name came from the initials of my grandchildren—JiKair Andre Delrico Danejah, DaSheay, Aram.

At the same time, I applied for new position at my job, which would have been a promotion for me, and after being encouraged to interview for the position, I was told that it wasn't quite time for me. In that instant I knew, my purpose there had been fulfilled, and I needed to focus on turning JADA House into a reality and have it become all that God intended for it to be, plus I needed to visualize myself doing it full time. It is here that I began to think about retiring.

Our first meeting was Wednesday, October 14th, 2014, with three women, myself, my mom, my chair, and one of my church members. I served a nice meal, and we talked amongst ourselves as we extended encouragement, prayers for families, communities, church, children, our world. These first three ladies grew to about twelve to fifteen in about three months.

My granddaughters helped me set up every Monday evening, one evening, they asked me could I start something for them—the teens. We began having teen night every Thursday in my home, again starting with three of us. My granddaughter started recruiting her friends. From three to thirteen females.

In the meantime, I continued growing in my spiritual walk. I went from being Deaconess to Minister Terri Shields.

JADA house began to pick up steam, and with the support of some knowledgeable women in the group, we expanded, and they gave me a lot of ideas that helped with our progress. Soon we begin hosting a back to school, backpack give away, which I named "Blast Off". We all pitched in and purchased backpacks, school supplies, raffle prizes, food, and beverages, and made sure we had music. We ended up giving away thirty-five back-packs with supplies. Our very first event was highly successful with a tremendous turnout.

Soon we added another event which was a senior luncheon which we hosted for the three senior high rises in our community. They were significant events as well, with speakers, music, and a lavish meal. The goal of this event was to honor our seniors and give them a few hours of just being loved on.

As we continued to expand our reach and attempt to make a difference in our community, I was financing all our activities. The evenings in my home with dinner I covered all the costs, from food to paper products—I enjoyed every bit of it. At the same time, we were getting noticed by individuals of note in our community. Staff members of our local politicians, folks involved with funder, and other people who saw value in what we were doing. Subsequently we were encouraged to apply for a 501c3 so we could acquire non-profit status thus allowing us to receive funds from foundations.

We remained meeting in my house for four years when God began opening doors for us that to this day continue to blow my mind. We caught the eye of key funders in this city. I met an amazing young man just by chance (of course I know God is not a "by chance" God, He is always placing people in your path at the right time) in a comic book-store of all places. As it turns out Zach Zefris was a grant writer. God just directed me to meet with this young man, three times, and Zach saw the vision, introduced me to my bookkeeper, and began writing grants for me—using my words, and boy did the funding began coming through.

This changed the game for JADA HOUSE INTERNATIONAL. We stepped up all our events, adding a layer of educational and health screening information. Also, most importantly we were able to move to a larger space outside my home that better meet the needs of our ever-expanding program.

My entire life has been one giant lesson: I managed to embrace each season and make it work for me. A part of that has been being able to be very instrumental in helping to shift the dynamics in my community. People began to see in me some of the same things that I imagine the judge who gave me probation instead of jail time saw. I became the chair of the Greater Hazelwood Collaborative an organization that brought all the factions together who are serving the community.

I am very proud of my community and of the role I was able to play, in the way we came together to make things happen in the Hazelwood community.

It is always significant when even as a seasoned woman, you keep growing. And I was doing just that and learning so much at the same time. I am pleased to say that I'm still knee deep in that growth and acquiring more wisdom as I go along. It has been my goal to make a difference in the lives of women who needed that space to be transparent and open about their need for healing, and/or sharing in general. Through JADA HOUSE INTERNATIONAL, I have attempted to do that. It has overlapped into other areas of service.

I pray that my life could be an example to younger women everywhere to realize three things: 1. Never give up. 2. Know for sure that God has a plan for your life as it says in Jeremiah 29:11 and 3. Don't listen to the negative chatter in your head – ever. If I had listened to that voice, there would be no JADA HOUSE INTERNATIONAL, no twenty plus years at a job that has allowed me to retire with a significant pension, and a paid in full home, and still remain relevant making a meaningful contribution to society. All because my latter is much more than my former, but for sure without my former. TLS

RENEE P. ALDRICH

Founder and Director, Softer Side Seminars,
Award-winning Writer
Pittsburgh, Pennsylvania

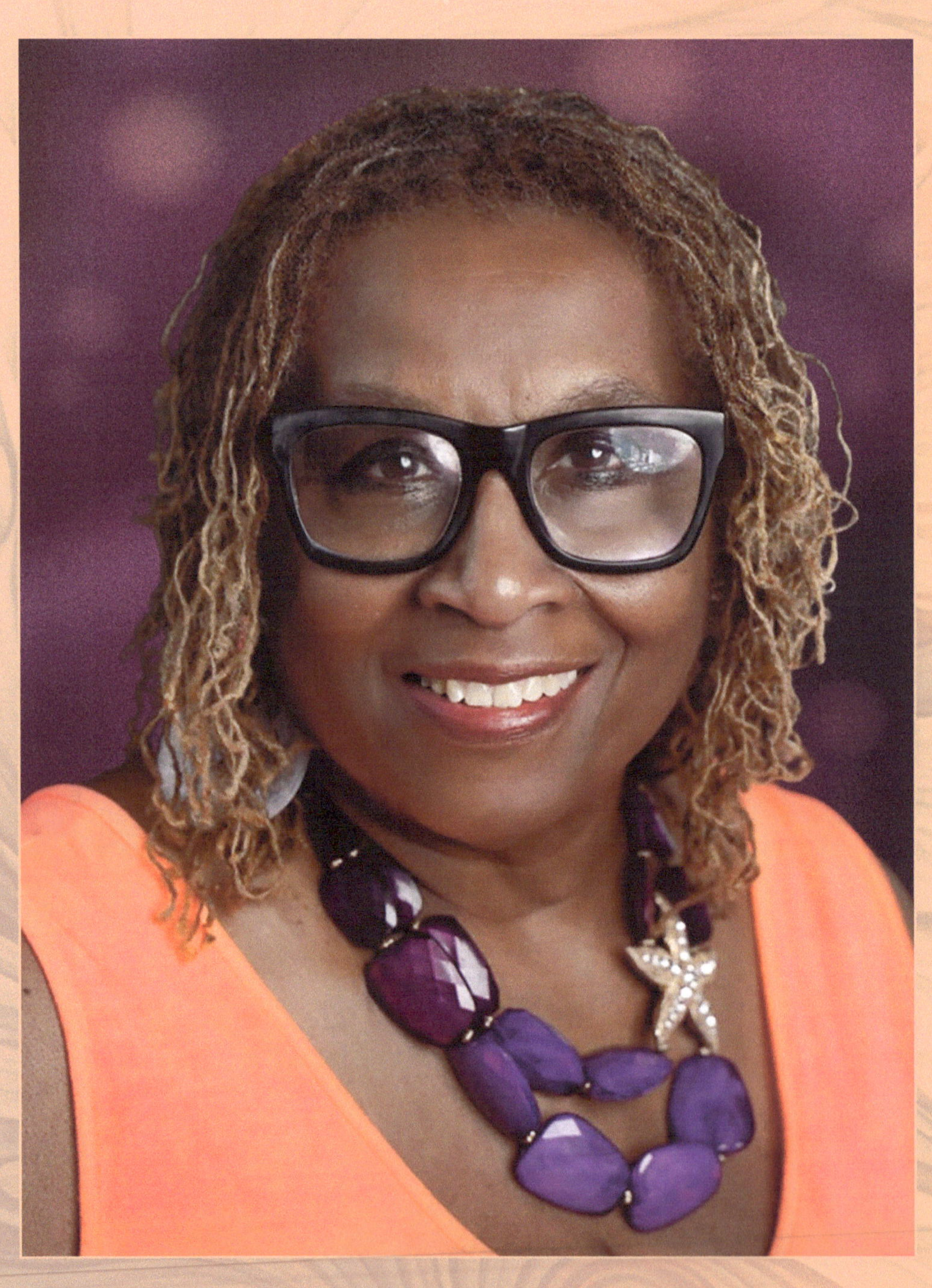

What's It All About—Aging?

The song, "Alfie," written by Burt Bacharach and Hal David in 1966, and of course popularized by songstress Dionne Warwick, (definitely a boomer song), was the soundtrack for the movie of the same name, begged the question, "What's it all about, Alfie?   Is it just for the moment that we live? What's it all about when we sort it out, Alfie? Are we meant to take more than we give? Or are we to \be kind?"

In this film, a handsome bachelor lives his life pursuing women. He wined and dined them, wooed them, and slept with them, then he dumped them and moved on to the next unwitting victim.   His philosophy was to do whatever you want to people and don't worry about the consequences—as long as you got what you wanted.   He did this throughout the film and even when he got a woman pregnant, his position was the same; after he had his way with her, he sees no reason to stay with her—he has gotten what he wants, and the baby was just an unfortunate by-product.

I've been hearing this song a lot lately, and I recalled the movie, and it made me think of the situation around senior Black women in this country. What it appears to be for us—Senior Women—is that in our youth, 20s 30s 40s, we are wined and dined, we are welcomed on jobs, in relationships, with advertisers, in our churches, in society period—when we have our youth and present a vivacious, and healthy demeanor, we are embraced, held close, adored, and the world is our playground. We are danced and led around the ballroom until we lost our glass slipper.

During this period, society is taking from us, but we have it all to give and don't really need much. Our skin and hair are beautiful, and we have boundless energy, so much so that we are able to leap tall buildings in a single bound. We are essentially super, and many times all the while having babies, raising toddlers, working a job, keeping a house, being wife or a girlfriend, and matching everyone's energy.

However, soon after we slip out of our 40s into our 50s, and though we still might look good, the energy is waning, and all of a sudden, the job offers slow up; it seems like industries are NOT seeking the wisdom we've acquired over the years, but instead are still looking for that effervescent energy—that is found in young and bouncy. Of course, then, while we were napping, we slipped past the age of 55. The symptoms of menopause come crashing down— heating us up when everyone else is cold, causing us to sweat viciously at night, and sending our emotions into a tailspin. Suddenly, we become fodder for late-night comedians, and society is losing interest in our viability for anything except for the sale of leaky pads and commercials highlighting our diminishing capacity. Not so much for men, though. We've all heard that when a man begins to age, he begins to look distinguished, while as women, we begin to look like a hag. —I'm confident I'm not the only one who has heard this. And with each passing year, it gets worse and worse – So the question for me is "What is it all About? - this Aging thing."

Sadly, the United States is the only country which does not honor its seniors. According to The Asia Health and Wellbeing Initiative (AHWIN ahwin.org/about-win) in an article in Economic Research Institute of ASEAN And East Asia And Japan Center For International Exchange, In Japan, seniors are at the top of their social hierarchy and the Japanese have a long tradition of respecting and caring for it's elderly. And boast a national holiday dedicated to older citizens honoring their contributions to society.

Norway, Sweden, Switzerland, Germany, and Canada are the top-ranking countries who honor their senior citizens; the United States and the U.K. fall somewhere below 15th place.

It is very telling for the U.S. when we are supposed to be the richest country in the world and have the most sophisticated resources for taking care of all ages. And if you are a Black senior woman in this country, regrettably, you truly are low on the totem pole but unfortunately high in the most critical places--health-- dying from heart disease, for one. According to Black Doctor.com, diseases of the heart and circulation, which include heart attacks, stroke, heart failure, kidney disease, hypertension, and diabetes, are responsible for killing more Black women than anything else in our society. Additionally, it is found in the same article, that "African American women are significantly negatively affected by heart disease. They experience higher mortality rates than White women and Black men under the age of 55 years. The mortality rate from coronary heart disease is 69% higher than for White women. In addition, the first heart attack occurs at an earlier age in Black women and is more likely to be fatal than is the case in White women. Premenopausal women who have hypertension, which is more common in Black women, have ten times the risk of heart attack than those without high blood pressure. These stats are not unlike the disparities in breast cancer—Black women may develop breast cancer less than White women. Still, because of late-stage diagnoses, there is a higher mortality rate in women of color than their white counterparts.

With all of the health issues we face, over which we have minimal control, it stands to reason that as a collective and individually, we should be more inclined to "rescue" each other from disparities that come from just living in a society that is NOT "user friendly" to women who are in their seasoned years. When I say "rescue," I mean being a part of the change we seek regarding eliminating the disdain senior women face. Let's make a personal commitment to be one who encourages instead of being a naysayer in our relationships with one another. I feel rescued when my peers encourage me to go back to school if that is a desire I express. I feel seen when my peers show respect for some unorthodox admission I may make.   And I feel honored when society recognizes the wisdom I bring to any situation and that they—society, my community, my family, the workplace—are made better because of me and my age. I feel respected when I am NOT treated disdain-fully nor looked at as diminished because I have crossed a certain age threshold in life.

When I consider the unmitigated facts, not only can I go back to school, at 70 I can start a business, or at 73, I can purchase a home, or travel solo to Africa, or even at 75, I can take up sky diving, or even finally write the great American novel.

Let's consider the words of Susan Sontag, who wrote:

"Women have another option. They can aspire to be wise, not merely nice; to be compe-tent, not merely helpful; to be strong, not merely graceful; to be ambitious for themselves, not merely for themselves in relation to men and children. They can let themselves age naturally without embarrassment, actively protesting and disobeying the conventions that stem from this society's double standard about aging. Instead of being girls, girls as long as possible, then age humiliatingly into middle aged women, they can become women much earlier – and remain active adults, enjoying the long, erotic career of which women are capable, far longer. Women should allow their faces to show the lives they have lived. Women should tell the truth."

When we master these concepts and embrace philosophies that uplift, we will then know "What's it All About – this Aging Thing." And answer the question long ago put to that rogue Alfie! RPA

ACKNOWLEDGMENTS

I want to acknowledge the ten brave women who agreed last year to participate in this project.

I appreciate your openness, the work, and the effort you had to employ to get this done. As a writer I know first-hand what it takes to get your thoughts on paper. I know what is involved in getting to a finished product that looks like it was oh-so-easy. But, the path to that end is, on many occasions, filled with a few pebbles along the way, and anyone will tell you that five-six tiny pebbles in your shoe can have the same impact as running blindly into a giant boulder.

SO THANK YOU, LADIES, WITH ALL MY HEART—I'll forever cherish this road we took together!! RPA

About the Compiler & Editor
Renee P. Aldrich

Renee P. Aldrich has been privileged to serve in various roles over the past 20-plus years. She's the founder and director of Softer Side Seminars, an empowerment and self-esteem-building program for women and girls. An award-winning writer, she is a published author of a companion book to Softer Side Seminars, Notes from the Softer Side, and has a freelance writing business, "Writing the Write Word." Ms. Aldrich has been named a New Pittsburgh Courier, Woman of Excellence and was the first prize winner for Creative Non-Fiction at Carlow University Creative Writing Department. She is a Pittsburgh Black Media Federation member, a commissioned poet, and a prose writer. Ms. Aldrich has found that the most important role she has held dear is mother to two adult children, Elliott James Lawrence of Long Beach, California, and Karen Cammille Aldrich of Pittsburgh, Pennsylvania, and grandmother to six–year old Karon Joshua Wingate.

www.ingramcontent.com/pod-product-compliance
Lightning Source LLC
Chambersburg PA
CBHW041410300726
48978CB00002B/42